What people are saying about …

IT'S YOUR CALL

"Gary Barkalow believes that you have a calling, and your calling makes you an artist. Read this book to discover the beauty of your art and the importance of yielding your artistry to God. For only the art of the Almighty artist can change the world."

Leonard Sweet, best-selling author of *Jesus Manifesto* (with Frank Viola), *Nudge,* and *So Beautiful*, and chief contributor to sermons.com

"Gary writes to remind all of us that God put us on this earth full of purpose. This very moment your life is full of potential, so don't waste a day, don't waste a year, don't waste your life."

Palmer Chinchen, PhD, pastor and author of *True Religion*

"Calling carries loads of misconceptions these days. Too often it is considered unique to the super-spiritual or synonymous with a lifelong carpet ride of ease and success. Barkalow gives apt treatment to these concepts; however, he also approaches calling from a far less peripheral sense—and one that is far more remarkable, I daresay. For thorough interactions with the personal, practical, and spiritual sides to a life of meaning and meaningful calling, this resource is first-class."

Abbie Smith, author of *Can You Keep Your Faith in College?* and coauthor of *The Slow Fade*

"I love this book. This is not a book that will tell you whether or not you are in the right job or doing the right thing. It is a book that will set you free to be yourself. In it, Gary gives us markers—not to figure out our lives, but to help us interpret our lives and discover who we were created to be. Gary is an artist, and in this book he invites us to live our passions with the same precision and practice with which he has honed his calling to … calling. I've read countless books on calling, but Gary's artistry with the subject draws me in, compels me to listen to God's way with my heart, and to live beautifully."

Jan Meyers Proett, author of *The Allure of Hope* and *Listening to Love*

"*It's Your Call* is a gift to all those who are seeking to know God and follow His call on their lives. Gary has been faithfully pursuing the Caller and His call for years, and his words give wisdom and insight. The power is not in the call, but in one's relationship with the Caller. Gary has learned a way of bringing the two together for empowered living. Read this book as if you were sitting with Gary, as I have, and take it in and go deep. It will change everything!"

Paul Stanley, coauthor of *Connecting* and former vice president of The Navigators

"Feeling stuck? Craving a life of purpose and meaning? Wondering what in the world you're destined to become? Gary Barkalow understands the frustration, confusion, and struggle that people face while trying to discover what God made them to be and do. Now he invites others to experience the joy of living a life that reflects God's glory. Packed with wisdom from Scripture and insights from sages, *It's Your Call* dismantles many stifling, limiting assumptions about calling and purpose and then leads us on a journey to become who we truly are."

Ann Kroeker, author of *Not So Fast: Slow-Down Solutions for Frenzied Families*

What Are You Doing Here?

IT'S YOUR CALL

What Are You Doing Here?

IT'S YOUR CALL

GARY BARKALOW

transforming lives together

IT'S YOUR CALL
Published by David C. Cook
4050 Lee Vance View
Colorado Springs, CO 80918 U.S.A.

David C. Cook Distribution Canada
55 Woodslee Avenue, Paris, Ontario, Canada N3L 3E5

David C. Cook U.K., Kingsway Communications
Eastbourne, East Sussex BN23 6NT, England

David C. Cook and the graphic circle C logo
are registered trademarks of Cook Communications Ministries.

The Web site addresses recommended throughout this book are offered as a
resource to you. These Web sites are not intended in any way to be or imply an
endorsement on the part of David C. Cook, nor do we vouch for their content.

LCCN 2010932062
ISBN 978-1-4347-6439-3
eISBN 978-0-7814-0575-1

© 2010 Gary Barkalow

The Team: John Blase, Amy Kiechlin, Caitlyn York, Karen Athen
Cover Design: Sarah Schultz
Cover Image: iStockphoto, royalty-free
Interior Photos: Alexie Patane, LexieMariePhoto.com

Printed in the United States of America
First Edition 2010

1 2 3 4 5 6 7 8 9 10

080510

DEDICATION

*My greatest hope, joy, fulfillment, and love emanate
from and around my family. Though I love what I
do and the friendships it has brought me, my greatest
love is for and from my family: my stunning wife,
Leigh, and my remarkable children, Alexie, Jesse,
Nick, Lacey, and now my son-in-law, Chris.*

*My boys once said to me, "Dad, I'm afraid to think
what you'd be doing and where you'd be living if
you weren't married to Mom." My thought was,
"Me, too." Leigh, you inspire me. I love you.*

*The completion of this book is a dream come true and a
cherished accomplishment, but my children are the fulfillment
of my greatest dreams and aspirations. I hope that what I have
learned over the years and have written in this book guides you
in your walk with God and into your truest desires. I love you.*

Contents

ACKNOWLEDGMENTS

I want to acknowledge several people for the weighty role they played in the completion of this book … and in my life.

Misty French, who edited and encouraged every chapter in this book before I sent it to the publisher.

John Blase, who picked up and ran with the idea of publishing this material with David C. Cook when I came to believe that no one would invest in this.

Bart Hansen, who fought for me through some of the toughest times and encouraged me not to give up on this book.

Tom Colwell and Kevin Miles, who insisted that this book could and would be published—and offered whatever was needed.

Paul Stanley and Brent Curtis, who poured so much of their glory into my life.

And to the "tribal chiefs" and my "brothers" who offered counsel and a warm fire for my heart and a timely war cry when it was needed.

I am grateful.

PREFACE

DEAR READER,

Let me introduce myself, because you are going to see a lot of my interior life as you read this. I'm not going to tell you primarily about other people's lives. Rather, I'm going to tell you about mine, because I don't think I'm very different from you. Writing a book on a subject doesn't mean you've done it right; it just means you've put your ideas, observations, and learning on paper.

Years ago, I ran across a statement from Oswald Chambers: "Soak continually in the one great truth of which you have had a vision; take it to bed with you, sleep with it, rise up in the morning with it. Continually bring your imagination into captivity to it and slowly and surely as the months and years go by, God will make you one of His specialists in that particular truth."[1] This is what I have done with the subject of *calling* for more than a quarter century. I'm not saying that I am an expert, but I would say I've become a specialist—someone who has intensely focused on a field of study. But you won't hear my voice only. You will hear the thoughts of many weighty people who have stood the test of time: C. S. Lewis, George MacDonald, Søren Kierkegaard, Dallas Willard, Oswald Chambers, Os Guinness, and more. A friend who read the manuscript said it felt like he was invited to listen in on a gathering of sages—people who had mentored me and were now asking me to contribute my observations and understanding on the subject. Perfect. That's what I want this book to be.

This is not your typical how-to, tips-and-techniques book. This book is not about what you can do, but about who you are. This is not about what you are good at, but what the good is that God has created in you. This is not about finding a job, but finding your life. This book is not about finding a solution to the situation you are in, but about deciphering your life as it unfolds in and around that situation. You see, your life is far deeper, far weightier than you have probably come to believe, and that is why all of the career, calling, or personality tests, assessments, and indicators have not helped a great deal or at a profound level. You are more than you have imagined, and there is more going on than you have probably been led to believe.

I want to encourage you to take your time with each chapter. What I have written, I have learned through more than twenty years of study, observation, conversations, reflection, and evaluation, so it will take more than several hours of reading to assimilate this. There is a lot here, and it is sequential—one thing builds on the next. This material is not about acquiring more knowledge; rather it is about gaining an experiential understanding of your life with God and what you're here for.

Gary Barkalow

Chapter 1

THE WEIGHTINESS
OF YOUR LIFE

CALLING IS THE MOST COMPREHENSIVE
REORIENTATION AND THE MOST PROFOUND
MOTIVATION IN HUMAN EXPERIENCE.
—Os Guinness

The truth is, I was jealous.

I was watching a nature show about lions in Africa. It was an amazing production following a lion's life from birth through adulthood. I watched the lion as a cub rolling in the grass, wrestling with his siblings, pouncing on his father, being groomed by his mother. As the cub got older, I watched him on his initial hunts—finding some success but mostly failure. In later life, he found a mate and had his own cubs. His days consisted of guiltlessly resting in the shade in the heat of the day, confidently hunting for food, and valiantly defending his family from predators. Something about the simple clarity of his life and his sense of "being"—untouched by the nagging questions of "who am I?" and "what should I be doing with my life?"—stirred something along the lines of jealousy in me. It wasn't necessarily a simple life I wanted, but rather his simple clarity. He was just being what he was ... a lion.

Can you relate to my jealousy? You know you're created to be something, to do something, to contribute something, but it's so hard to figure out what that something is.

In C. S. Lewis's The Chronicles of Narnia we read of a great prince imprisoned by a witch's sorcery. Under her spell, Prince Rilian would lose all recollection of who he was and where he came from—"While I was enchanted I could not remember my true self."[1] During his brief moments of clarity (though the witch told him that those moments were actually times of insanity), the prince would be involuntarily bound to a chair until he would come back into his "right mind," which he later described as a "heavy, tangled, cold, clammy web of evil magic."[2]

I believe this is how life feels for most of us; we're lost in a fog of confusion and dullness with only brief moments of clarity and desire that seem so hard to hold on to. And when we are able to capture those moments that have a ring of authenticity about them, we quickly start to doubt their legitimacy. Could we be under some web of evil magic? Some spell?

We live in a time that is brutal on a person's search for purpose or place in the world. The world of science tells us (with a voice of reason and certainty) that, whatever we feel—be it pleasure, despair, anger, lightness, heaviness, or even a sense of meaning—these emotions are just a series of chemical reactions in our brain to some outside stimuli. Beauty, purpose, meaning, romance, pleasure, and even God are nothing more than by-products of chemical reactions. Science tells us there is no meaning or transcendent purpose in life, only the random reaction of one thing to another. As philosopher and Nobel Prize winner Henri Bergson believed,

> *Since the Renaissance, modern science has gradually extended its causal explanations to one phenomenon after another, psychological and biological as well as the purely physical, accounting even for life and consciousness in purely physical or chemical terms. Creative novelty, human purpose, and freedom have often been disregarded.[3]*

Then we have society, largely encountered through laws and media, which tells us that any sense of purpose or meaning outside the realm of economic or scientific advancement is unhelpful and dangerous. Laws portray society's desire to separate faith from any type of cultural influence. And most movies, TV shows, and news reports show religious conviction as ignorant and the source of hatred, suffering, and war—or, at best, ineffective for positively changing the world.

And what about the church? In the past, the church held an elitist view of people and their callings, where only a few were chosen to do something sacred. These select few could be easily recognized by their religious title, position, or clothing. If you did not have the desire or opportunity to do something within the church, your life's work was not of eternal consequence. Your expected position in life was simply to subject yourself to the church's teaching and direction, with your highest goal being to live a moral life and to support the church's vision and institutions. But I want to state clearly: There is no "elite" group in the body of Christ.

More recently the church has adopted a utilitarian view of man, focusing on usefulness. There is much to be done for the kingdom of God, so we need to be a servant, to be dutiful, to do whatever needs to be done. And thus the commonly heard expression: "I just want to be used by God." When you attach this phrase to another relationship such as a friend or pastor, or a situation such as a work environment or marriage, something surfaces in our hearts revealing how unhealthy or undignified this way of thinking really is. This life on earth and your relationship to God are about so much more than your usefulness.

And lately the church has added on a stewardship view of life, the thought being that God has given us something to contribute to His kingdom work, something by which we will be scrutinized and judged. The unstated goal here is not to get in trouble on our job evaluation. I believe God has instead given us something glorious to bring to this world that has to do with joy and intimacy with Him, not a forthcoming job evaluation.

Everybody's Question

Several years ago I ran across an article in *USA Today* in which adults were surveyed as to what they "would ask a god or supreme being if they could get a direct and immediate answer." The largest percentage (34 percent) of adults said they would ask, "What is my purpose in life?" Second (19 percent) and third (16 percent) to that question were, "Will I have life after death?" and "Why do bad things happen?"[4]

That most commonly asked question is very telling. It demonstrates that we were created for a specific purpose. As C. S. Lewis said, "If the whole universe has no meaning, we should never have found out that it has no meaning: just as, if there were no light in the universe, and therefore no creatures with eyes, we should never know that it was dark. *Dark* would be a word without meaning."[5] So the question we are all asking—"Is there a specific purpose or calling for my life?"—is self-answering: YES!

The Barna Research Group concluded a nationwide survey with these words: "One of the most stunning outcomes was that born again Christians and non-Christians were equally likely to be seeking meaning and purpose in life."[6] Barna was also amazed that so many born-again Christians were puzzled as to their purpose in life: "One of the primary values of the Christian faith is to settle the issue of meaning and purpose in life. The Bible endorses people's individual uniqueness but also provides a clear understanding of the meaning of life—that being to know, love and serve God with all of your heart, mind and strength."[7]

The question of purpose, meaning, and place is universal to every human heart. The answer that your life does have purpose or meaning is not enough. Instead the answer begs another question, "What specific, irreplaceable purpose does my life play?" Coming to faith does not settle the issue of meaning and purpose in life. As Pulitzer Prize winner Russell Baker said,

> *There is a hunger in us...for assurance that our lives have not been merely successful, but valuable—that we have accomplished something grander than just another well-heeled [well-off], loudly publicized journey from the diaper to the shroud. In short, that our lives have been consequential.[8]*

The truth is that we are here to do something, a contribution that only each one of us can make. There is an outcome that hinges on us and therefore a fear that we might miss it—our moment, our part, our potential, our purpose, and our life. This is not some peculiar fear experienced only by a certain generation or culture or religion. I believe it is a fear born out of a desire written on every human heart, a desire for meaning, to know that my existence matters to someone and something. In short, that I'm good for something.

The hunger or desire to find and live the life that we have been given, to live a life that is consequential, is good and noble. Scripture says, "[God] will give eternal life to those who keep on doing good, seeking after the glory and honor and immortality that God offers. But he will pour out his anger and wrath on those who live for themselves, who refuse to obey the truth and instead live lives of wickedness" (Rom. 2:7–8 NLT). There *is* a life of glory, honor, and immortality that God offers and that we are meant to seek. But it will take God's help for us to find and live the life we were created to live.

> NOW WITH GOD'S HELP I SHALL BECOME MYSELF.
> **—Søren Kierkegaard**

TOO EASY, TOO HARD

We have been raised in the modern scientific era, where our culture has tried to reduce life down to its essence, to a fundamental formula to explain and replicate everything. This is as true for calling as it is for health, finances, relationships, and parenting. As a result, most of us settle for describing our personality or "strengths" in terms of letters like "High D" or "ISTJ" or as an animal like "Golden Retriever."

As is often the case, this has spilled over into the church. We can now state our spiritual gift(s) because we've used an assessment tool or been given a prophetic word by someone "in the know." It all seems so authoritative and affirming. But as many of us have discovered our "passions," we've realized an absence of joy. We experience a sense of guilt for feeling so little about the list of what the "truly spiritual" should care most deeply about. It all just feels so foggy. If it's really so easy to find our calling or purpose, why does it feel so hard? Why don't these methods work, really work?

THE MYTH OF UNDERSTANDING

Unfortunately, we have equated understanding with attainment. In the academic world, you learn the required material and attain your degree. But life is not always academic; it's often much deeper. Understanding the components of a good marriage does not make one. Understanding the principles of money management does not keep you out of debt. Understanding the techniques of a good golf swing does not get you closer to the green. Understanding the practices of healthy living does not keep you healthy. In the same way, understanding your complexities or propensities will not necessarily usher you into a meaningful, purposeful life.

There is a depth—what I call a *weightiness*—to your life that cannot be released or entered into by way of testing, analysis, goal setting, or determination. Understanding alone, or as the primary approach, cannot do the job. Have you found this to be true? Have you tried some of the tests, indicators, surveys, formulas, and processes that have been offered in the last several decades, but here you are, reading yet another book, hoping for some meaningful clarity and purposeful movement toward your calling in life?

Most of the various twentysomethings I have met with over the years have been disheartened, if not immobilized, by the expectation that after graduation they should know exactly who they are and what place they have in this world. Some have been assaulted with Luke 12:48: "From everyone who has been given much, much will be demanded; and from the one who has been entrusted with much, much more will be asked." Fearfully, shamefully not knowing who they are or what is being required of them, these beautiful young people take on the life scripts that others have handed them, defining what they should do and how they should live their lives. A friend moved to Washington DC to take a public policy job on the recommendation of an older man because the man spoke with a confidence and excitement about what my friend could accomplish for the kingdom of God. The job and the environment literally almost took my friend's life—emotionally, relationally, and spiritually.

Or, like a hiker lost in the wilderness with a GPS unit, there are those of us a little older who've attempted to find our place in life using the coordinates of salary, position, and advancement. After several years in the military in a rather prestigious job, Ted felt that something needed to change vocationally. Having retired, he then felt pressure to quickly find the "right place" for the next season of his life. However, having little knowledge of who he truly was, even though he had been given a great deal of personal assessment (outplacement) data, he had no idea in what direction he should go. Ted accepted a position with a large international company that offered him a fast-track program to a top position with a high salary. After years of relocating from one city to another, doing work he did not enjoy or value, Ted resigned and once again sought to find the "right place" that would lead to the fulfillment of his calling in life. He realized that he was searching for guidance using the wrong coordinates.

When Jesus referred to something being "given" (Luke 12:48) to us, was He referring simply to assets? Assets like education, training, money, possessions, skills, and influence—things that for the most part can be acquired? Or could He have been referring to something much deeper, something more *weighty,* that God offers us?

MISLEADING COORDINATES

Years ago I took my kids out camping in a part of the Colorado wilderness. One morning we set out to reach a high point that we could see from our campsite. After an hour or so of hiking and climbing we reached the summit and took in the spectacular vistas. Then, before starting back, we visually located our campsite and identified several landmarks to guide us back on our descent. What I did not realize at the time was that the rock outcroppings I was using as markers were inadequate for guiding us to our destination. Though they were part of the landscape, they were not specific enough to our campsite. Walking toward these markers actually distanced us from our destination.

In the same way, there have been two misleading ideas by which people have tried to navigate, ideas that have taken them off course in the pursuit of their calling. The first is that your calling or purpose is to find the right job (paid) or position (unpaid). This idea is treacherous for a couple of reasons. For one, this puts your calling in the hands of another (i.e., some level of corporate, church, or nonprofit leadership). Over my years of working in the nonprofit-ministry realm, I have had many individuals tell me they were called to a position in my area. In other words, I was the gatekeeper to the fulfillment of their purpose in life. Now if I had the power to give them their calling by offering them a job, then it was just as true that I had the power to take it away. How can something be required or asked of you that you do not have influence over? Your calling or purpose is not determined by the mood or opinions of those in authority, or by the job market, or by the current economic situation. I have heard too many people use these circumstances as excuses for living small, unfulfilled lives.

Your calling cannot be fully contained and fulfilled by a job or position. How could the weight of your life be defined by a list of functions or tasks? In almost all jobs, after a while you kind of "get the job down" to the point that you can do it without thinking, most often halfheartedly. The purpose or calling of your life will require *all* of you—a wholeheartedness.

While I was managing a gymnastic center in Southern California, I had a locksmith come in to fix one of the doors. Halfway through his repair work I asked him if he enjoyed his work. He said, "No, I could train a monkey to do what I do." He hated the fact that his job really didn't require much of him, at least not anymore. It wasn't lost on me that a locksmith, someone usually with "the keys," had come to a place of complaining, discontentment, a loss of creativity, and distraction (always looking elsewhere). He was locked out of the life he wanted to live—which is where many of us end up living.

Second, if finding your calling is tied to finding the right job or position, your calling would be limited to the extent of that work. In a typical job, your life's purpose would be limited to forty hours a week. Or if you believed your calling was to a position such as a Sunday school teacher, your calling would be limited to perhaps one hour a week. What do you do then with your life's purpose the remaining hours of the week? Does your life not count during those "off" hours? Is your life split somewhere between the mundane and the sacred?

While some have been misdirected by the idea that finding their calling is finding the right job, others have been sidelined by the belief that their calling is to be like Jesus. After all, the Bible says, "For those God foreknew he also predestined to be conformed to the likeness of his Son" (Rom. 8:29). Just what exactly does it mean to be like Jesus? For many people, being like Jesus is simply being moral. Is that all Jesus was—moral? Was that the purpose of His life on earth? There was far more to Jesus' life than being sinless. Jesus said, "I have come that they may have life, and have it to the full" (John 10:10). Jesus came with a mission, a purpose—to bring life to others. In His first public statement about the mission of His life, He read from Isaiah 61: "He has sent me to bind up the brokenhearted, to proclaim freedom for the captives and release from darkness for the prisoners.... [And they will become] oaks of righteousness ... for the display of his splendor" (vv. 1, 3). Jesus' life, as well as yours, is not about the absence of something (sin), but rather the presence of something (a splendor or weightiness).

So are we to be like Jesus? Absolutely! But His morality is not to be our goal. As the apostle Paul said, "I press on to possess that perfection for which Christ Jesus first possessed me" (Phil. 3:12 NLT). Jesus was a man of purpose and passion, and we are to be transformed into His image: "God knew what he was doing from the very beginning. He decided from the outset to shape the lives of those who love him along the same lines as the life of his Son. The Son stands first in the line of humanity he restored" (Rom 8:29 MSG). Your calling is much more than moral behavior.

SAGELY PERSPECTIVE

Counselor and author Richard Leider asked senior citizens over a twenty-five-year span how they would live their lives differently. Across the board, the older adults say the same things:

First, they say that if they could live their lives over again, they would be more reflective. They got so caught up in the doing ... that they lost sight of the meaning.... Second, they would take more risks.... Almost all of them said that they felt most alive when they took risks.... Third ... they would understand what really gave them fulfillment ... doing something that contributes to life, adding value to life beyond yourself.[9]

These responses remind me of Moses' prayer: "Teach us how short our lives really are so that we may be wise" (Ps. 90:12 NCV).

Reflection

There is a direction, theme, purpose, and orchestration to our lives that we must recognize and understand if we are to discern the lives we were created to live. It is important that we periodically disengage from our daily busyness and examine our lives. If we are to truly "see" and "hear" our lives, we must get away from all the ambient light and noise, as we would if we were seriously studying the stars.

Oswald Chambers wrote, "Looking back we see the presence of an amazing design, which, if we are born of God, we will credit to God. We can all see God in exceptional things, but it requires the culture of spiritual discipline to see God in every detail. Never allow that the haphazard is anything less than God's appointed order, and be ready to discover the Divine designs anywhere."[10]

We must cultivate the spiritual discipline of reflection, seeing God's choreography in our lives.

Risk

We all desire a life that requires something from us, not just our "showing up." It's exhilarating to attempt something that is risky, uncertain, *and* important. I have heard it said that the most spectacular vistas require traveling the roughest, most dangerous trails. And so it is with our lives—to reach the most beautiful, authentic, fulfilling places in life will require some risk. A life lived in fear is a life half-lived.

Theodore Roosevelt said,

> *It is not the critic who counts; not the man who points out how the strong man stumbles, or where the doer of deeds could have done them better. The credit belongs to the man who is actually in the arena, whose face is marred by dust and sweat and blood, who strives valiantly; who errs and comes short again and again; because there is no effort without error and shortcomings; but who does actually strive to do the deeds; who knows the great enthusiasms, the great devotions, who spends himself in a worthy cause, who at the best knows in the end the triumph of high achievement, and who at the worst, if he fails, at least he fails while daring greatly, so that his place shall never be with those cold and timid souls who know neither victory nor defeat.*[11]

Fulfillment

All of us instinctually want to know that there is meaning to our lives and that we add meaning for those around us—that we are living a life of consequence and transcendence. Elton Trueblood wrote, "A man has made at least a start on discovering the meaning of human life when he plants shade trees under which he knows full well he will never sit." We want to live for something more than ourselves. Meaning and fulfillment are only experienced as our lives, in some way, touch another person. Those who live solely for themselves— *their* needs, *their* happiness, *their* comfort and protection—will suffer a claustrophobia of the heart, the acute discomfort of living in a story far too small. A person's heart is as large as the things he loves.

So, possessing a calling (a weighty purpose in life) is not just for a few—the "elite." It is the design and destiny of every person. If there was not great meaning to our lives, we would not be asking questions about our calling. A life of calling is by no means limited to the categories that we have been given: church, missionary, public office, the "professions." Nor could our calling be fully contained, utilized, or fulfilled in a job or position. The calling on our lives is as broad, as large, as grand as the story we are living in. The creative scope of our calling is, as Dallas Willard put it, to live as a "co-worker with God in the creative enterprise of life on earth." Our calling is about something deeper, something more profound and pervasive than any assessment, test, or indicator could ever fully touch or grasp.

I believe most of you reading this are with me so far. But here is where the questions arise: *How do I navigate these unfriendly, confusing waters of calling and purpose? What coordinates should I use? How do I become my true self? How do I find my passion and purpose?* I want to invite you to come along with me as we walk forward with the intent to live out the answer to the question we're all asking—*what am I doing here?*

Chapter 2

THE MYSTERY
OF YOUR LIFE

LIFE CAN ONLY BE UNDERSTOOD BACKWARD;
BUT IT MUST BE LIVED FORWARD.
—Søren Kierkegaard

Several years ago my family was given the gift of a week at a dude ranch. It was seven days of horseback riding, great meals, hilarious skits, square dances, and a rodeo competition. We loved it. During our time at the ranch, we got to know a couple from England. Over one of our dinner conversations, I asked this couple what they dreamed of doing when they retired in two years. They both answered without any hesitation and with great excitement, "Sail around the world in our sailboat!"

Not knowing anything about sailing, I asked why. Again, without hesitation and with smiles on their faces, they started telling me sailing stories. They talked about the thrill of being on the open water at great distances from land and the adventure of weathering violent storms. After hearing this, my question intensified—why would anyone want to experience something like that voluntarily? It was clear this couple loved the sea—it *called* to them. They had some type of relationship to the sea that I did not have. I was reminded of Oswald Chambers' words: "The call of God is like the call of the sea, no one hears it but the one who has the nature of the sea in him."[1] I do not have the nature of the sea in me, so I cannot hear its call as the couple from England did. Their excitement, their desire, their call to the sea was completely foreign to me.

If you know God personally, through the work of and belief in Jesus Christ, then you have the nature of God in you. If you have God's nature in you, then you can also hear the call of eternity, transcendence, meaning, and the unique desires that have been placed in your own heart. Only you can hear them.

Definitely Not Definitely

Chambers went on to say, "It cannot be stated definitely what the call of God is to, because His call is to be in comradeship with Himself for His own purposes, and the test is to believe that God knows what He is after."[2]

We tend to look for a definitive activity, position, or place that we can call "God's will" for our lives. We want a precise, easily under-standable answer to the question, "What am I supposed to do with my life?" But we are never offered that in Scripture. What Scripture does say is that God "will instruct you and teach you in the way you should go" (Ps. 32:8) and that He "is producing in you both the desire and the ability to do what pleases him" (Phil. 2:13 ISV). God's calling on our lives is far more mysterious than methodological, and mystery is something we don't handle very well.

The mystery in our lives surfaces in questions like:

> I've always loved photography ... what does that have to do with my life and work?

> I was perfect for that position ... why was I not chosen?

> Why has this person come into my life?

> Why does everything in my life seem to be on hold right now?

> Why hasn't God intervened in this situation?

> Why does this keep happening?

"Beyond all question, the mystery of godliness is great" (1 Tim. 3:16). We have gone through the modern era of science and reason, which is not favorable toward or tolerant of mystery. Mystery has been seen as the lack of applied intelligence and effort and therefore a sign of ignorance. As a result, many have come to hold mystery in contempt.

But even the apostle Paul, having been given insight into the mystery of Christ (Eph. 3:3–4), said, "All that I know now is partial and incomplete, but then I will know everything completely, just as God now knows me completely" (1 Cor. 13:12 NLT). Since this was true of Paul, then we can relax a bit not knowing everything about our lives and calling.

The tension, as Søren Kierkegaard wrote, is that "life can only be understood backward; but it must be lived forward." The understanding that we gain by looking back on life is invaluable (which we will explore later on in this book), but it will not answer all our questions regarding our intended future.

It is my intent to lessen the burden and pressure we place on ourselves for understanding or clarity. Mystery is something to be embraced, journeyed through, and enjoyed. It's not that mystery can never be explained but rather that mystery unfolds—not all at once, but a little at a time.

"Oh, the depth of the riches of the wisdom and knowledge of God! How unsearchable his judgments, and his paths beyond tracing out! 'Who has known the mind of the Lord? Or who has been his counselor?'" (Rom. 11:33–34). God is not a little confused or in the dark. He knows what is going on, who you are, and why you are here at this time in His story. We must believe that God knows what He is after with us.

In the midst of mystery it is helpful to remember that "the best is perhaps what we understand least."[3] There is more to you than you know. What is most glorious about you is yet to be fully revealed. Your life has a depth and purpose that cannot be revealed in a moment in time; it must be journeyed into with one discovery leading into the next.

The English writer Jonathan Swift said, "It is, in men as in soils, where sometimes there is a vein of gold which the owner knows not of."[4] Though mystery shrouds the glory of our lives, it is there. Mystery must be mined, one shovelful at a time, and with careful inspection of each collection. It is easy to overlook gold when your eye is not trained for the unpolished mineral.

> ALL THAT IS GOLD DOES NOT GLITTER, NOT
> ALL THOSE WHO WANDER ARE LOST.
> **—J.R.R. Tolkien,** *The Fellowship of the Ring*

Why does there have to be mystery? If you think about it, there's no way we can comprehend the immensity of creation and life. Heck, I can't comprehend how grass can grow in the cracks of my sidewalk but not in certain parts of my lawn that I take care to water and fertilize. But there are reasons mystery is essential in our lives. One is found in Proverbs 25:2: "It is the glory of God to conceal a matter; to search out a matter is the glory of kings."

AN INVITATION TO JOY

God loves to hide things. Not so we won't find them, but because of the joy we will experience in the search and discovery.

When our children were younger, we would hide plastic Easter eggs filled with jelly beans around the house. My wife, Leigh, and

I had a blast deciding where to hide the eggs so that it would take some effort to find them but also so they could be found. Our greater joy was watching our kids discover the Easter eggs with shouts of "I found one!"

One of the thrilling joys in life, at any age, is to discover something that you've been searching for—from discovering what's preventing you from balancing your checking account to finally finding something that you're good at and enjoy. These revelations usually come in part by something inherent in our nature: to be curious. We certainly were curious when we were younger. For many of us, our curiosity was pushed aside by practicality and busyness, making mystery an annoyance rather than an adventure. Much of our lives is designed to be navigated by curiosity.

Albert Einstein is quoted as saying, "One cannot help but be in awe when he contemplates the mysteries of eternity, of life, of the marvelous structure of reality. It is enough if one tries merely to comprehend a little of this mystery every day. Never lose a holy curiosity."[5]

Just so you don't think I'm making too much of one obscure Old Testament verse, Jesus said the same thing in Matthew 7:7–8: "Keep on asking, and you will receive what you ask for. Keep on seeking, and you will find. Keep on knocking, and the door will be opened to you. For everyone who asks, receives. Everyone who seeks, finds. And to everyone who knocks, the door will be opened" (NLT).

Sadly, most of us don't ask, seek, or knock very often or for very long. We ask God what He is up to, who we are, or what He wants us to do usually when we are in some sort of crisis. We will stick with these types of questions until the confusion, stress, or pain stops. It may be several hours or several days. If the situation is severe enough, we may pursue God for several weeks. But once the crisis is over, it's like we slip back under a spell.

Oswald Chambers said, "We will long and desire and crave and suffer, but not until we are at the extreme limit will we ask...until you get to the point of asking you won't receive from God. To receive means you have come into the relationship of a child of God, and now you perceive with intelligent and moral appreciation and spiritual understanding that these things come from God."[6] Jesus tells a story just before His "ask, seek, and knock" statement that explains possibly the most overlooked element of our searching. He tells of a man who goes to his friend's house late at night to borrow some food to feed an unexpected guest. His friend, irritated at the audacity of the inopportune request, shouts through the door, "No!" But because his friend was *persistent*, literally bold and shameless, he was given what he was searching for.

We are not to occasionally ask, seek, and knock. Our life is to be one of continually asking, seeking, and knocking. We are to be explorers not tourists, archaeologists not museum visitors. Our life should be continual shouts of "I found another one!"

AN INVITATION TO INTIMACY

Not only does God want us to experience the excitement of discovering truths about our purpose and design, He wants us to stay in intimate conversation with Him. God knows that if He were to tell us everything we needed to know about our lives, assuming we could comprehend it, we would probably run off in desire and excitement to fulfill our purpose, without returning to the conversation.

I believe God will give us enough clarity to keep us encouraged and moving, but He will also shroud enough of our purpose in mystery to keep us coming back for more intimate conversation. God loves when we come back to Him, with our heart, for more. He says, "'For I know the plans that I have for you,' declares the LORD, 'plans for welfare and not for calamity to give you a future and a hope. Then you will call upon Me and come and pray to Me, and I will listen to you. You will seek Me and find Me when you search for Me with all your heart'" (Jer. 29:11–13 NASB).

Mystery is an invitation to intimacy with God. Instead of wasting your energy fighting mystery, allow mystery to stir you and guide you to keep asking and seeking and knocking.

UNDERSTANDING OR GOD

> AS THINKERS WE ARE CUT OFF FROM WHAT
> WE THINK ABOUT; AS TASTING, TOUCHING,
> WILLING, LOVING, HATING. THE MORE
> LUCIDLY [RATIONALLY, LOGICALLY] WE THINK,
> THE MORE WE ARE CUT OFF.... YOU CANNOT
> *STUDY* PLEASURE IN THE MOMENT OF THE
> NUPTIAL EMBRACE, NOR REPENTANCE WHILE
> REPENTING, NOR ANALYZE THE NATURE OF
> HUMOUR WHILE ROARING WITH LAUGHTER.[7]
> **—C. S. Lewis**

We say something similar today in the phrase "Don't lose the moment." We don't want to lose the experience of an important moment by disengaging our hearts through analysis or distraction. Lewis's marital example is so clear—if you reduce intimacy to clinical techniques, you're sure to lose the beauty of that magical moment. You can attempt to have understanding, or you can have your mate.

One evening after a men's conference, I took Leigh out on a dinner date to ask her some questions about her level of happiness with our marriage and life. I was actually fulfilling an assignment from the conference. Sitting across from her, I covertly pulled out my Day-Timer with the assigned questions, laying it open by my leg. Throughout the evening I asked her one question after another until she leaned forward and asked, "Are you reading these questions?" I've never been able to hide anything from Leigh. I expressed that I loved discovering these things about her, but the questions were suggested by the speaker at the men's conference. Grabbing my hand, she said, "I would rather have your heart than these questions." I had lost the moment. In my attempt to understand, I had lost the very person I was looking for—Leigh. Please hear me: Understanding is a good and needed thing, but it can be gained in different ways.

One of the things I enjoy doing is trap shooting (shooting clay pigeons with a shotgun). Some days I'm fairly accurate hitting a high percentage of clays, and other days I can't seem to hit anything. On those "off" days, if I get all worked up with "why am I missing all these shots?" and "I've got to figure out what I'm doing wrong," I'm doomed to failure and disappointment. But I've learned that if I can simply take the pressure off of trying to find an answer and enjoy the activity, I will usually start to shoot more accurately. In other words, aiming for the *experience* of trap shooting rather than understanding allows me to reach my goal.

We can work so hard for understanding in our circumstances that we lose the purpose and experience of it, not to mention God's presence within it. Understanding comes to us more fully after the event, upon reflection; so what we must do during the event is stay fully engaged. A friend and mentor, Paul Stanley, told me that we don't learn from experience—we learn from evaluated experience. It's hard to evaluate an experience that we were absent from at a heart level.

Driven by the need for an immediate answer to the question "What should I do right now?" or "Why is this happening to me?" we put a great deal of pressure on ourselves, and we narrow our range of hearing. God may want to speak to some area in our lives or in our relationship with Him, but we are unable to hear because we are only open to a *particular* conversation.

Preferring the Deep, Resisting the Shallow

I spent my high school years and my college summers in southern Florida. Though I do not have the "nature of the sea" in me, I do love to snorkel and scuba dive. I remember driving along the beach, seeing people play in the shallow surf, and thinking, *Why don't they go out into the deeper waters where the real fun, beauty, and adventure is?* I'm sure that many of these people had settled for the shallows because they weren't sure they could handle the deeper water and were afraid of what might be out there. But they were missing so much—they were too much in the "land world," and therefore they were missing the "underwater world." I am quite certain the deeper waters held what they were really looking for.

It's the same for us as followers of Jesus Christ. We stay in the shallows of Christianity—in smaller, safer, more understandable and controllable stories where we "know what we are doing." But we find few answers there to the deeper questions about who we are and what our place in this world really is.

One day, after Jesus had finished speaking to a crowd on the seashore, He said something a little out of left field—Jesus began telling a professional fisherman how to fish: "He said to Simon, 'Put out into deep water, and let down the nets for a catch.' Simon answered, 'Master, we've worked hard all night and haven't caught anything. But because you say so, I will let down the nets'" (Luke 5:4–5). Simon could have said something like, "I spent all night out there.... There is nothing out there for me.... It's too much work, and I'm tired of disappointment." But instead, to his credit, Simon went out into the depths.

He found the very thing he had been looking for, which had previously eluded him ... and not only that; he found more than he thought possible: "When they had done so, they caught such a large number of fish that their nets began to break. So they signaled their partners in the other boat to come and help them, and they came and filled both boats so full that they began to sink" (vv. 6–7).

As spectacular as that miracle was, Simon was about to discover something far more grand—he was about to discover the very thing that he was created to do: *big-game fishing*. Simon was so astonished by what Jesus had obviously done that he fell at His feet when he got to shore. Jesus said to Simon, "Don't be afraid; from now on you will catch men" (v. 10).

Many of us wrestle with understanding the way chosen for us simply because we resist the deep (mystery), preferring the shallow instead. It is only as we embrace and journey into mystery that God will reveal who He is, who we are, and the realities of His kingdom.

RECOGNIZING GOD IN THE MYSTERY OF YOUR LIFE

Frederick Buechner wrote, "There is no event so commonplace but that God is present within it, always hiddenly, always leaving you room to recognize him or not to recognize him, but all the more fascinatingly because of that, all the more compellingly and hauntingly…. Listen to your life. See it for the fathomless mystery that it is. In the boredom and pain of it no less than in the excitement and gladness."[8]

God will even conceal Himself in the mystery of our lives so we will seek Him and then experience the incomparable joy of finding Him. It is the thrill expressed in Buechner's words: *fascinatingly, compellingly,* and *hauntingly.*

God is there with new revelations about our calling in all of our moments—in the times when we feel most alive, free, and ourselves as well as the times when we feel unfulfilled or hurt or lost. He is always whispering to us, "For I know the plans that I have for you … plans for welfare and not for calamity to give you a future and a hope…. You will seek Me and find Me when you search for Me with all your heart" (Jer. 29:11–13 NASB).

So, as Oswald Chambers said, "It cannot be stated definitely what the call of God is to, because His call is to be in comradeship with Himself for His own purposes." God's calling on our lives is far more mysterious than methodological. We want clarity, and what we most often get is mystery. But mystery should not be avoided or disdained—it is actually both a source of joy and an invitation into intimacy with God. God said that He "will instruct you and teach you in the way you should go" (Ps. 32:8) and that He "is producing in you both the desire and the ability to do what pleases him" (Phil. 2:13 ISV). The discovery of what God has created us to do is a matter of asking, seeking, and knocking. The discoverable clues about who we are can be found only as we resist the shallows and prefer the deep. We are to be explorers and archaeologists, not tourists and visitors.

Chapter 3

FINDING YOUR ORIENTATION

THERE IS NOT A HEART BUT HAS ITS MOMENTS OF
LONGING, YEARNING FOR SOMETHING BETTER,
NOBLER, HOLIER THAN IT KNOWS NOW.

—Henry Ward Beecher

I had just left a job, a place, and a community where I had been for seven years and thought I'd be for the remainder of my life. I knew why I needed to leave and what I wanted to do, but I wasn't sure how to get there. During this time, while walking into a hardware store, a friend called me. I stood just inside the automatic doors for twenty minutes while Jeff told me a story that related to my current situation. Jeff, who had been a commercial airline pilot, explained to me one of the procedures that had to take place between the ending of one flight and the beginning of the next. While the Boeing 757 sat at the gate exiting its passengers and refueling and preparing for its next load, its navigational computer had to clear the past maps and errors and recalibrate for the new course. In order to do that, the plane had to sit completely still for ten minutes while it reestablished true north—otherwise its navigation would be dangerously off. This recalibration was an issue of orientation—to the geographic North Pole while factoring in the rotation of the earth.

While standing in the hardware store, I came to understand that Jeff was a messenger of God for my life that day. And I found that Jeff's encouragement, along with my wife's (who had been telling me the same thing), was a part of my own recalibration process during this new leg of my journey. The point was that I needed to sit still with God for a while so my heart could recalibrate to my true north—finding its orientation to the movement of God in my life.

ORIENTATION

I was a competitive gymnast for ten years. The greatest enemy I faced was not fear or pain or injury, though they were formidable. They could be overcome. The greatest adversary was disorientation, from which there was no quick recovery. I would train for hours to learn a particular skill—watching videotapes and dissecting the move into every action the body had to take, determining what strength and flexibility would be required and what I would see, either with my actual eyes or in my mind. And then, once I could perform the skill, I would practice it again and again until I could do it "without thinking." But every once in a while, in the middle of a gymnastics routine, I would lose orientation—my sense of up and down, left and right. At that moment all of my skill, strength, and training were useless. In these dreaded moments nothing would make sense, and all I could do was brace for the crash. I hadn't lost my skill or strength; I had lost my surroundings, my positioning, and my context. I was lost.

In a state of disorientation, our lives do not make sense. Little pieces of information gained through tests, assessments, and indicators really don't help much. Knowing your tendencies or strengths isn't helpful or hopeful in finding your place when you don't even know what's going on around you.

GPS AND TRIANGULATION

I've always been fascinated with GPS (global positioning systems) devices. It amazes me how these little devices can communicate with satellites that are 13,000 miles (20,967 kilometers) above us and then orient us to where we are in the world to within a few feet. The thing that caught my attention a few years ago when I purchased a GPS unit was that there must be at least three coordinates, three satellites by which to triangulate, in order for the GPS to give an accurate location.

I believe in order for us to navigate at least fairly accurately to our place in this world, to our calling, we must continually triangulate using three reference points: story, desire, and journey.

Story

David Whyte, author of *The Heart Aroused,* said, "Work is drama, and our inability to live vitally upon its stage has ... much to do with the modern loss of dramatic sensibility, the lost sense that we play out our lives as part of a greater story."[1] What a great phrase! That we would be keenly aware of God's Greater Story, oriented to our lives and to our place in the story.

I believe we live in a story that is much larger than we have ever realized. More is going on, more is at stake than we have been told. Our role is more significant than we have come to believe. Something dramatic is going on.

A classic Mother Goose rhyme conveys the significance, consequence, and irreplaceability of our lives in this Greater Story:

> *For want of a nail*
> *The shoe was lost,*
> *For want of a shoe*
> *The horse was lost,*
> *For want of a horse*
> *The rider was lost,*
> *For want of a rider*
> *The battle was lost,*
> *For want of a battle*
> *The kingdom was lost,*

And all for the want
Of a horse shoe nail.

This poem speaks of the significance of what appear to be just ordinary, mundane life chores (making nails and shoeing horses) determining the outcome of a great battle between kingdoms. There is something big going on, something that you are here to do: a contribution that only you can make, an outcome that hinges on you.

Have you ever walked into the middle of a conversation and tried to quickly enter in by offering your thoughts, only to realize you shouldn't have? And did it occur to you that you had no idea what was really going on or what was really needed? Of course, we all have—and hopefully we have learned to be "quick to listen, slow to speak" as James 1:19 instructs us.

Or on a more significant level, have you ever made a determination about a situation or person that seemed so crystal clear, so obvious, until you discovered that there were other things going on—other factors? One person seems so aloof, so discourteous because they haven't returned your phone calls or emails, until you find out how overwhelmed they are with a family or work issue. Or you were sure that your boss or your pastor was inconsiderate and self-serving because of a decision he made that hurt others, until you realized all he had to wrestle with, that something had to be done, that someone was inevitably going to be hurt and he would be painfully misunderstood. This is why we are encouraged not to be naive: "The naive [simple minded] believes everything, but the sensible [perceptive] man considers his steps" (Prov. 14:15 NASB).

There is always a context, a setting, a story. Perhaps you have heard the expression: A text without a context is a con. It's true.

We misunderstand situations, others, our own life when we simply take the "text" of the moment without understanding the context, the Greater Story that is going on. As the old adage goes—there is always more going on than meets the eye.

Jesus brought this up with a group of people who were having a hard time with the direction of His life because, as they were trying to read the text (what they saw and heard) of His life, they did not understand the context.

> *[Jesus] said to the crowd: "When you see a cloud rising in the west, immediately you say, 'It's going to rain,' and it does. And when the south wind blows, you say, 'It's going to be hot,' and it is. Hypocrites! You know how to interpret the appearance of the earth and the sky. How is it that you don't know how to interpret this present time?" (Luke 12:54–56)*

This was not Jesus demeaning their ability to read atmospheric conditions. Jesus was saying that, just as you have learned how to read the story of the sky, you must also learn how to read the story of the kingdoms. The crowd was reading the text and the appearance of His life but remained oblivious to the context, the setting for Jesus' life. The masses were trying to hand Him a script, a role that they believed He was to play out. And He refused it:

> *I have come to bring fire on the earth, and how I wish it were already kindled! But I have a baptism to undergo, and how distressed I am until it*

is completed! Do you think I came to bring peace on earth? No, I tell you, but division." (Luke 12:49–51)

Maybe you've experienced something similar to this. The crowd around you—your church community or your extended family—was sure about the life you were to live. But in the moments of escape from the pressure, you knew somehow this was not really you.

Then there are the more potent moments when a significant, well-meaning, caring individual suggests what you ought to do with your life. Peter did this with Jesus:

> *Jesus began to tell his disciples plainly that it was necessary for him to go to Jerusalem, and that he would suffer many terrible things at the hands of the elders, the leading priests, and the teachers of religious law. He would be killed, but on the third day he would be raised from the dead.*
>
> *But Peter took him aside and began to reprimand him for saying such things. "Heaven forbid, Lord," he said. "This will never happen to you!"*
>
> *Jesus turned to Peter and said, "Get away from me, Satan! You are a dangerous trap to me. You are seeing things merely from a human point of view, not from God's." (Matt. 16:21–23 NLT)*

Many have been handed scripts for their lives by well-meaning people who were good at reading the environment but didn't understand the world they were living in. We have accepted their scripts and pursued education, training, jobs, vocations, and opportunities that we didn't care much about, nor did we enjoy.

If I took you into Blockbuster and asked you to find a story that best represents the story you are living, in what section would you start looking: action and adventure, drama, comedy, sci-fi and fantasy, animation, horror, family and kids, mystery and suspense, romance, documentary, war? The reason I ask is because the story you believe you are living determines how you interpret and react to life.

Let's imagine you've just stepped onto a cruise ship for the vacation of your dreams. Your expectations are high—you have picked the best-rated cruise liner, the best destinations, the best weather possibilities, and you've paid a premium price. Shortly after the cruise begins, the weather changes from cloudless skies and calm seas to wind, rain, and turbulent water. The changing conditions have taken some of your desired activities and freedoms away. You are now forced indoors for most of the time and are relying on the food and amenities to make up for what was taken from you. You are disappointed by the service, which seems unreasonably slow, and the food, which is not as fresh and hot as you expected. All of the other people, who are also seeking shelter from the weather, are invading your space—they are needy and loud and too numerous. Even when you retreat to the sanctuary of your cabin, you can still hear their voices and their clunking around. You find yourself shouting (at least under your breath), "Why do things have to be like this; why do things have to be so hard; why can't You come through for me, God—at least once?"

Now let me simply change the setting of this story. You are boarding a ship, but it is not a vacation cruise liner; it is a battleship.

You have dreamed of and worked hard for this day. Your expectations are high—to be in the company of other warriors playing a significant part in a great battle for the lives and freedom of others. It's crowded, but you are glad you're not alone and you know that you need each other. The food isn't great, but it sustains you. Life fluctuates from boredom to intensity, but you know you are moving toward the objective. The conditions outside may be rough, but you hardly notice because you're focused on your role, your job, your contribution on the ship, and your preparation. You find yourself shouting (at least under your breath), "When do I get to do what I was trained to do; when do I engage the enemy?"

All I did was change the story line. In the first story, the theme was rather small—personal comfort, enjoyment, peacetime: vacation. In the second story the theme was large—great mission, transcendence, a time of war: the battle for freedom and life.

Most of us live under the illusion of the first story, while assenting to the reality of the second story. As believers, we say we understand that there is a great battle between the kingdoms—the kingdom of God and the kingdom of Satan. But we live as if we were civilians and believe the battle to be an unthreatening distance away. And so we have made our mission the quality of our lives and the controlling of external factors. We have made our lives about being on a vacation cruise liner, rather than about realizing we are on a battleship heading toward a great mission.

UNTIL WE RECOGNIZE THAT LIFE IS NOT JUST
SOMETHING TO BE ENJOYED BUT RATHER
A TASK THAT EACH OF US IS ASSIGNED,

WE'LL NEVER FIND MEANING IN OUR LIVES
AND WILL NEVER BE TRULY HAPPY.
—Victor Frankl

*

The Theme of the Greater Story: Overcoming and Becoming

Part of the Greater Story is in our "becoming" who we were created to be. It must be so, for "it is only when the man has become his name that God gives him the stone with the name upon it, for then first can he understand what his name signifies.... Such a name cannot be given until the man *is* the name."[2]

The other part of this Greater Story is in our "overcoming." And if overcoming is a requirement, then there must be forces to prevail over, enemies to conquer. We must live as if we are in a battle with very high stakes; this is our story.

Overcoming and becoming. It is the theme of the story we live in. Nikolai Berdyaev said, "Living the good life is frequently dull, flat and commonplace. Our greatest need is to make life fiery, creative and capable of spiritual struggle." If he is right, and I believe he is, then God has our lives covered—and our lives are a fiery, creative, spiritual struggle.

A Significant but Lesser Story—Our Story

So we live in, as David Whyte wrote, "the modern loss of dramatic sensibility." We must get back this sense-ability by orienting our lives to the larger unfolding reality. In order to do this, we must also be aware of our own developing story—the story of our becoming. As we take inventory, as we examine the screenplay that has already been written and played out, we can begin to understand the intentions of the Author—to discern what He may be up to. Our story reveals His themes. God always builds on what He has already done.

We need to be aware of the defining moments throughout our lives; the people that entered our story and their deposits or withdrawals; the moments when we were most alive and the times we felt wholly lost; the things we have dreamed about and the things we most feared; the stories and the toys we loved as children. All of these various aspects and themes are a part of our unfolding story and are meant to bring revelation to who we are. They are not random and trivial quirks; they are *you*.

Dan Allender said, "Stories don't give answers, but they do offer perspective." In order to find our place in this world, our calling, we need to have perspective—orientation. But story is only one reference point by which we triangulate. We also need to orient our hearts to desire.

Desire

George MacDonald wrote, "With every man God has a secret." God's secret with you is who you are—your character, your nature, and your meaning. Although the full and final description of our lives will be given on a future day, God is progressively revealing the answer: "The path of the righteous is like the first gleam of dawn, shining ever brighter till the full light of day" (Prov. 4:18).

Scripture says, "[God] will point them to the best way.... The LORD tells his secrets to those who respect him" (Ps. 25:12, 14 NCV). As we walk with God, He will reveal to us His secret about our created design and His intention for us, for our path. But how? Where?

What you were created to do is revealed in the form of your desires. As we've already seen, "It is God who is producing in you both the desire and the ability to do what pleases him" (Phil. 2:13 ISV). You see, the really great news is that what you are supposed to do is what you most want to do! I may need to repeat that: What you are supposed to do is what you most want to do! Or as Os Guinness wrote, "Instead of, 'You are what you do,' calling says: 'Do what you are.'"[3]

I realize this may sound foreign and dangerous, maybe even blasphemous to you. The church doesn't talk much about desire, at least not in a positive way. After all, people have done some pretty stupid, selfish, and harmful things all in the name of desire. Much of the talk around the subject of calling tends to center around need and obligation and naturally heads in the direction of duty. But we are to live out of desire, not duty. As C. S. Lewis noted, "A *perfect* man would never act from a sense of duty; he'd always *want* the right thing more than the wrong one. Duty is only a substitute for love (of God and of other people), like a crutch that is a substitute for a leg. Most of us need the crutch at times: but of course it is idiotic to use the crutch when our own legs (our own loves, tastes, habits, etc.) can do the journey on their own!"[4] We are invited to live out of desire, but desire is often messy and hard to understand. I will say much more about this in the chapters to come, but for now it is critical to know that God has and will continue to tell you what you are here to do through your desires.

With the orientation of story and desire, we are close to being able to triangulate our purpose in this world, but in order to do this we need the third reference point: *journey.*

Journey

If we fail to remember that there is a process, a progression, a journey that every person must take, we will misinterpret and misunderstand life.

Years ago, I went on a five-day backpacking trip into the Colorado backcountry. I had not done any real backpacking before, so all I could picture in my mind was staying in campsites, cooking meals, having conversations around a campfire, and sleeping in a tent. I had no idea what backpacking would take in terms of strength, endurance, and time; I didn't understand that significant effort was required to experience beauty and adventure. I was poised for a rude awakening and overwhelming dismay. But several of the men I was traveling with walked me through the realities of this journey in terms of daily distances, time on our feet, altitude gains and losses, proper equipment, nutritional needs, backpack weight, and climate changes. Consequently, my expectations changed, and I acquired what I needed for the trip in terms of equipment, supplies, and physical conditioning. Being aware of the journey, not just the destination, made all the difference in the experience.

Scripture says, "Blessed are those whose strength is in you, who have set their hearts on pilgrimage. As they pass through the Valley of Baca, they make it a place of springs; the autumn rains also cover it with pools. They go from strength to strength, till each appears before God in Zion" (Ps. 84:5–7).

We are on a pilgrimage—a long journey to a sacred place for a sacred purpose. We will pass through many places and through many seasons: weeping and drought, joy and abundance. Ultimately we will go from one level of strength to a greater level of strength, which can only come from God.

Scripture also says, "We, who with unveiled faces all reflect the Lord's glory, are being transformed into his likeness with ever-increasing glory, which comes from the Lord, who is the Spirit" (2 Cor. 3:18).

Our lives are to be the progressive transformation from one level of glory to a greater level of glory. Transformation always takes time, but time does not always bring transformation. Transformation into something greater takes a pilgrimage.

When Jesse, my older son, graduated from high school, he decided to go on a pilgrimage—a historic, literal pilgrimage. The journey is known as the Way of St. James, a pilgrimage to the Cathedral of Santiago de Compostela in Galicia in northwestern Spain, where tradition holds that the remains of the apostle James are buried. Jesse started along the French border of Saint-Jean-Pied-de-Port, crossing the Pyrenees mountain range into Spain and walking five hundred miles (eight hundred kilometers) to Santiago de Compostela … alone. Though he had studied the route and the reports other pilgrims had written, the journey held more hardship, beauty, and adventure than he had anticipated. Forty-five days later, Leigh and I stood at the Denver International Airport waiting to see Jesse emerge from the escalator after his flight home. At the very first glimpse him, we could see that transformation had taken place. The change wasn't anything physical; it was something in his countenance—he had aged, or better yet, he had "increased." Not because forty-five days had been added to his life, but because of what he had journeyed through.

As with the subject of desire, I will say much more about the subject of journey in coming chapters.

If we stay alert to the three reference points of story, desire, and journey, we can triangulate our location and our role in the Greater Story. We can be oriented—Alert and Oriented Times Three (A&Ox3).

A&OX3

Permit me to use another metaphor with these three reference points. When an EMT (emergency medical technician) or paramedic comes upon a trauma victim, one of the first things he or she will do is assess level of consciousness. To do that, the trauma victim will be asked three questions: *What is your name? What day is it? Where are you?* If these three questions are answered correctly, then the trauma victim is considered to be fully conscious—Alert and Oriented Times Three. We also must be fully conscious—alert and oriented to our story, our desire, and our journey.

A fourth question has now been added to the protocol, establishing what is known as Alert and Oriented Times Four (A&Ox4): *Can you tell me what happened to you?* This same question gives us another reference point essential to finding our calling: revelation.

REVELATION

We need to know certain things in order to walk in our calling, which cannot be revealed by the wisdom that comes from an awareness of story, desire, and journey. These particulars must be revealed to us by God. This is why Paul wrote that he prayed that God would "give to you a spirit of wisdom and of revelation in the knowledge of Him ... that the eyes of your heart may be enlightened, so that you will know what is the hope of His calling" (Eph. 1:17–18 NASB). Wisdom (A&Ox3) and revelation (A&Ox4).

Remember, what we need to know but don't at this moment is mystery ... and mystery is God's invitation to increased intimacy with Him.

Jesus said, "He who belongs to God hears what God says" (John 8:47). He also said, "I am the good shepherd; I know my sheep and my sheep know me.... My sheep listen to my voice; I know them, and they follow me" (John 10:14, 27). As Dallas Willard wrote,

> *God being who he is, and now revealed in the person of Jesus Christ, we should be surprised if he did not speak to us.... It is simply beyond belief that two persons so intimately related, as indicated by Jesus in his answer to Thaddeus (John 14:23), would not speak with each other. The Spirit that inhabits us is not dumb, restricting himself to an occasional nudge, a brilliant image, or a case of goose bumps.[5]*

God must speak ... because He promised to "instruct you and teach you in the way you should go" (Ps. 32:8).

We must listen because we are to be His followers and disciples. As Scripture says, "[God] wakens me morning by morning, wakens my ear to listen like one being taught" (Isa. 50:4).

Hearing God is a vital part of our walk with Him. I cannot do justice to this "intellectual and spiritual 'hard-hat area'" as Dallas Willard calls it. So, I want to encourage you to read Willard's book *In Search of Guidance: Developing a Conversational Relationship with God.*

So, if we are to find our calling, the intention of our lives, we must become oriented—we must find our true north. We must clear from our navigational equipment (our hearts) the inaccurate, invalid maps and errors and triangulate to the three universal coordinates: story, desire, and journey.

Story: We must continually remember that more is going on than we can see (there is a Greater Story), the stakes are higher than we've been told (we live on a battleship, not a cruise liner), and we are far more than we believe (we are the only ones, in the spiritual realm, who underestimate the power of our lives). The theme of this story is overcoming and becoming.

Desire: The great news is that what you were created to do in the Greater Story is what you most want to do—it is written on your heart in the form of your desires: "It is God who is producing in you both the desire and the ability to do what pleases him" (Phil. 2:13 ISV). We must also continually be aware, not only of the story we are living in, but of our desires.

Journey: In addition, we must always remember that there is a process, a progression, a journey that all people must take in becoming who they truly are and in recognizing the role they are to play.

And we must remember, as essential and powerful as these reference points are, beyond them there are things that only God can reveal about our lives. God wants to be intimately involved in our journeys of becoming, and because of His desire for our lives to become what they were destined to be, He must and will speak to us personally.

Chapter 4

THE GLORY
OF YOUR LIFE

For as long as I have been a Christian I have heard it said that I need to take responsibility for my sin—the weight, depth, and consequences of it. And while owning our sin is a part of walking with God, for "godly sorrow brings repentance that leads to salvation" (2 Cor. 7:10), Jesus said, "Repent *and* believe the good news!" (Mark 1:15). As Jesus read from Isaiah 61, the good news is that the brokenhearted can be healed, those in bondage can be set free, ashes can be exchanged for beauty, mourning for joy, and despair for praise. This is truly good news, but the Scripture does not end there. It says that those who repent and believe the good news will display God's splendor; they will rebuild, restore, and renew what was devastated and ruined.

OWN THE SPLENDOR OF YOUR LIFE

Because of the work of Christ for you and in you, you are now a revelation of God's splendor, His image bearer. You are not simply an object of God's forgiveness and tolerance, which is what most people believe about their lives. No, there is a brilliance, a magnificence to your life that you are to take responsibility for: the splendor of your life—not simply what has been taken away, but what has been given to you. C. S. Lewis said, "Redeemed humanity is to be something more glorious than unfallen humanity."[1]

There is something much truer about you than your need for and the granting of forgiveness. You started from a higher place. There is something more important, more heroic, more glorious about your life than you ever imagined. David says that God made us a little lower than Himself and has crowned us with glory and honor (Ps. 8: 5).

Let's pause a moment. Is that what you've come to understand? Do you live each day with an awareness and ownership of your glory and majesty? Probably not. I'm guessing this is not what you have been told, nor how you usually feel.

I would like to define the word *glory* for you—or perhaps redefine it. I came to know Christ in my college years in Georgia.

Between the underexplanation and overpronunciation of the word (*gloooooory*), *glory* was a mysterious and somewhat distasteful word to me. But this word is crucial for our understanding of God, of His creation, and of ourselves. *Glory* literally means the splendor, abundance, beauty, brilliance, or weightiness (importance) of a thing or person. David gazed at the stars and said that God's splendor, beauty, and brilliance is clearly seen in His artistry: "The heavens declare the *glory* of God; the skies proclaim the work of his hands" (Ps. 19:1). In the book of Proverbs we read that the glory (splendor, abundance) of young men is their strength and the glory of older men is their experience and wisdom (Prov. 20:29). When we see something beautiful—a picture, a sunset, a snowcapped mountain range—we call it *glorious*. We observe someone completely engaged in and enjoying an activity, and we may say they are "in their glory." Interestingly, we don't usually say that about a person who is simply doing something well; no, that description is reserved for those moments when we catch someone doing something beyond the level of fulfilling a function. Not something ordinary, but something extraordinary.

Here are a few examples. For instance, my wife and oldest daughter, Alexie, are phenomenal dancers. It only takes a certain type of music to get them moving. I have watched them dance in worship settings with other women, and the contrast in effect is astounding. Watching some of the other dancers, no matter how well they danced, I mostly felt their effort, their concentration, and their work. But watching my wife and daughter, I felt their enjoyment, their passion, and a sort of fully engaged thoughtlessness. Dance flows out of them from a place deeper than training. When they dance, they are in their glory. There is a splendor and abundance of dance in them. When they dance, they are extraordinary.

Then there's David, who served on a board of directors with me. David is certified in the area of human-resources management. His input and perspective, along with the others on the board, was invaluable for the board's function of governance. But during one particular board meeting something changed, and we all noticed it. David had a "knowing" about him, an uncommon engagement in the moment, a persuasive authority in his countenance and words that went far beyond his training. In that moment, he was in his glory. There was a weightiness to his life and words. Then and there, he was extraordinary.

And then there was the day I found one of my sons in the garage building something. He was oblivious, or at least unconcerned that he was being observed. He was totally engrossed in his work and enjoying every minute of it. My son was not even aware of the conditions surrounding him—the amount of light in the room, the temperature, or his hunger level. Something was going on in him beyond just having fun, something extraordinary. There was an importance, a weightiness, a splendor to his activity. He was in his glory.

In all of these examples, I experienced the "weightiness" of another's life, and it left an impression on me. I witnessed something extraordinary (outside the ordinary), something exceptional. These were not simply jobs well done; these were displays of each person's splendor and God's.

What I am trying to describe is not some extravagant, inappropriate truth about people—like an exquisite piece of art in a dreadful home. Knowing the glory God has put in us is vital to understanding how we have been redeemed, transformed, sanctified, consecrated, and made new.

In the Old Testament, we are told numerous times that God and His glory (His splendor, abundance, weightiness) inhabited the temple or tabernacle of His people. In the New Testament, after the intervention of Christ, Paul made it critically clear that nothing has changed except that *we* are now the dwelling place of God and His glory:

> *Don't you know that you yourselves are God's temple and that God's Spirit lives in you? (1 Cor. 3:16)*

> *For we are the temple of the living God. As God has said: "I will live with them and walk among them, and I will be their God, and they will be my people." (2 Cor. 6:16)*

Jesus said that His mission on earth was to restore us to our original purpose: to be a display of God's glory (Isa. 61:3), crowned with glory and honor (Ps. 8:5). And God, speaking to the forces that were oppressing His people, said,

> *"I will say to the north, 'Give them up!' and to the south, 'Do not hold them back.' Bring my sons from afar and my daughters from the ends of the earth—everyone who is called by my name, whom I created for my glory, whom I formed and made." (Isa. 43:6–7)*

So we were created to display God's glory. But how does a person do that? It's not easy, but it is simple: We live in and live out the splendor God has uniquely given us. We own the glory of our lives. We live out the extraordinary-ness in the ordinary things of life.

Norman Cousins said, "The tragedy of life is not death; rather, it is what we allow to die within us while we live." Have you allowed the splendor, beauty, abundance, brilliance, weightiness of your life to die? That would be truly tragic and detrimental to the world.

Scripture tells us that all of heaven waits with great anticipation to see if we will discover, own, and offer the splendor that God has given us: "Since we are surrounded by such a great cloud of witnesses, let us run with perseverance the race marked out for us" (Heb. 12:1). This "race marked out for us" is about something far weightier than our church attendance, giving, or volunteerism. It's about the world experiencing the aspect of God's glory that you carry.

It's that important!

You Underestimate the Weightiness of Your Life

By now, I would suspect that some degree of uneasiness is rising in you, some suspicion of blasphemy, sacrilege, fleshly pride. Of course, for we have grown up with ideas like, "I'm just a sinner saved by grace." Is that it? Nothing has changed in us or about our lives except for our forgiveness? Or, "My job is to get out of God's way." Really? We are nothing more than a nuisance, a hindrance, and a liability to

God? Or how about, "This is simply preparation for heaven"? You mean that my life really doesn't count here and now? Everything going on in this life really doesn't matter?

These are easily and widely accepted thoughts because they contain an element of truth and the hint of humility. But they are neither fully true nor the fruit of biblical humility. They are instead misapplied, out-of-context truths with the malicious intent of causing a person to disbelieve and disown the weightiness of his or her life. I'm not attributing malicious intent to the individuals or institutions you may have heard this from, but rather to the one who most fears your life—the Adversary of God, Satan. Because as we've seen before, the only one who underestimates the power of your life in the spiritual realm ... is *you*.

These ideas about the insignificance of our lives and our roles in this world have turned gloriously and powerfully redeemed people into passive, disengaged, acquiescing, faithless (practically speaking), disheartened individuals. It's understandable. So often, the deepest desires of our hearts are discounted. We have been encouraged to wear this false cloak of humility, believing that there is no splendor, beauty, or weightiness to our lives—that the more we dislike our lives on this earth, the greater the degree of our servanthood and the greater the purity of our love for God.

So the (church) culture has gone from the mysterious-but-true glory of a person's life to lifeless duty and function. It has gone from owning the splendor of one's life and the world's need of it to merely finding a task that "needs to be done" for God and making sure it is done with "excellence." The first requires intimacy with God and your whole heart; the latter does not.

As Jesus said to those who had missed the point of Scripture, "You are mistaken because you don't know the Scriptures or God's power" (Matt. 22:29 ISV). And so we see men and women working with/for Christian organizations and churches because they want to be "used by God" or "be a part of something big." But instead of experiencing a sense of fulfillment, joy, transcendence, adventure, beauty, and intimacy with God in their work, they find it disappointing and life-taking. As a friend of mine who worked for a Christian ministry and then attended a Christian graduate school said, "My calling was used up by the first and beat up by the second."

In the large Christian organizations I worked with, I often saw individuals on whom the prod of policies and punishments was used to inspire hard work or those who would work hard in a position ill-fitted for their glory until their heart gave out. Several physicians have told me that the greatest percentage of their clients dealing with depression or stress-related illnesses were employees of ministries. You know instinctively that there is something wrong with this.

Jesus said, "Take my yoke upon you, and learn from me, for I am gentle and lowly in heart, and you will find rest for your souls. *For my yoke is easy [or pleasant], and my burden is light*" (Matt. 11:29–30 ESV). You see, we are pilgrims in this world, and pilgrims travel lightly but with great purpose.

Eugene Peterson translates these words of Jesus as, "Walk with me and work with me—watch how I do it. Learn the unforced rhythms of grace. *I won't lay anything heavy or ill-fitting on you.* Keep company with me and you'll learn to *live freely and lightly*" (MSG). When we are living in our glory, what we do will feel "easy" and "light" though our circumstances may not.

CALLING, ROLES, AND ASSIGNMENTS

Your calling is to let the world around you experience the glory of your life. Made in the image of God (Gen. 1:27), every human being has a calling … a glory to their lives, though perhaps marred and enslaved. It is for this that Jesus came—to heal our hearts and set us free from what imprisons us so that we would become a display of God's splendor (Isa. 61:3–4).

A significant part of the effect of our lives on this world is the way we have loved our parents, spouse, children, friends, and coworkers, as well as the way we have worked in the home or in the marketplace. But these are roles, not a calling. I am a husband because I am married, a father because I have brought children into the world, an employee because I have chosen to work for someone. These are roles that I have taken on because of choices I have made.

I have had people tell me that they were called to be a husband or wife, a father or mother. As much as I appreciate the seriousness and significance they are giving to these responsibilities, they may be hiding from their calling. It's like the student who stays in the university system for six, eight, or ten years, not because he or she needs the high-level degree to do what they know they are here for, but precisely the opposite. They have no idea who they are and what they are to do, so they hide behind the role of student.

God also gives us assignments—to individuals, groups, or places that need our particular splendor, brilliance, abundance, or where we will receive needed training. For some it may be primarily at home with children—for others, in an organization or corporation, paid or unpaid. Whatever the assignment, it is given to us to help fulfill our roles and calling. For God will not require both from you and put them in opposition to each other. So, when an opportunity presents itself that needs the glory of our lives but will detract from our roles or that pays well but doesn't require the essence of who we are, we need to seriously pause and ask God if it is an assignment, a distraction, or just a rogue opportunity.

By staying aware that life consists of our calling, our roles, and our assignments, we can be free from the fear of having to create a career path or being stuck in a field of work/experience or limiting titles. We can move as God directs us and as our lives change, take the effect of our lives wherever we go. This is living in your calling.

The Inescapability of Your Glory

A young man named Joseph had a vision, a picture of his role in the Greater Story. In his youthfulness, Joseph shared this picture of his destiny with his brothers with little or no understanding of what it meant or of its process or timing. The jealousy, misunderstanding, and anger of his brothers set into motion a series of events that seemed to take Joseph away from his calling to rule over a kingdom.

At first, Joseph was a servant in the household of an officer of the king and the captain of the royal guard. "His master saw that the Lord was with him and that the Lord gave him success in everything he did" (Gen. 39:3). In other words, he spotted Joseph's glory, which he recognized as God-given. So Joseph's boss put him in charge of everything he had—to rule over his household.

Then in another turn of events, Joseph was sent to prison on false charges. There the warden spotted Joseph's glory and put him "in charge of all those held in the prison … [making him] responsible for all that was done there" (v. 22). He was now ruling over a prison.

In still another turn of events, the king asked Joseph what he should do about an impending famine. Upon receiving his counsel, in recognition of Joseph's glory, the king made him second in command: "Since God has made all this known to you, there is no one so discerning and wise as you. You shall be in charge of my palace, and all my people are to submit to your orders" (41:39–40). Joseph was now ruling over a kingdom.

The vision Joseph was given in his youth was a picture of the glory of his life *and* his final destination. His calling or glory was not a position, title, or place, but rather his extraordinary ability to see what was needed in a situation and to do it. Joseph lived in and out of his glory wherever he was. He couldn't help it; it was who God had made him to be. Joseph's choice to live this way is reminiscent of the apostle Paul's words, "I am compelled.… Woe to me if I do not" (1 Cor. 9:16).

As I have looked back on my life and done a kind of EKG (an electrocardiogram to diagnose heart activity) on my soul, I have discovered that throughout my life I have instinctually moved toward finding clarity (what's this all about?), focus (what's my or another's role in this?), and design (what needs to be put in place for this to work?). It was what I loved most in my years as a competitive gymnast—understanding what was required in a performance on the various pieces of equipment, discerning how to acquire and develop each element (skills, strength, balance, precision, flexibility), and choreographing each element into a unique routine. This is what I most enjoyed and how I most significantly contributed to running a gymnastics center and then a sports team ministry.

Clarity, focus, and design: These are what I brought to my work with nonprofits, my work in staff development, and now speaking, writing, and developing The Noble Heart Ministry. My understanding of these things was not something that I acquired through education or that circumstances required. It's not a matter of IQ (intelligence quotient), but of GQ (glory quotient), for your glory is your real genius!

These three things are simply what I have been compelled to bring to any situation or person throughout my life. They are what I have to "turn off," not what I have to "turn on," and they are what I naturally start looking for when I meet with a person or deal with a task.

A woman named Agnes Bojaxhiu reached the end of her lifetime having created a missionary order, hospitals, schools, orphanages, youth centers, and shelters for the world's most destitute. Quite an entrepreneur, a real visionary, a "go-getter," a humanitarian opportunist, right? She probably knew what her calling was and went after it, starting her climb up the religious ladder as she entered the order of the Sisters of Our Lady of Loreto in her quest to become the founder and CEO of a world-renowned missionary effort.

No—Agnes simply lived in and out of the beauty and abundance of her life: an extraordinary compassion for the unwanted, unloved, and uncared for. This is what drew her into teaching in one of the poorest areas of the world: Calcutta, India. And it was in that setting that, as she gazed over the walls of the convent, her heart was compelled to live in the middle of the impoverished and dying.

Though Agnes was moved by the poverty of circumstance and body, her heart was compelled by the poverty of the soul: "The greatest poverty is to feel unwanted and unloved." She did not live and work out of a sense of guilt, blatant need, or duty. Nor was it her strategically determined and highly trained skills that touched people so profoundly. It was her glory that impacted people, that elicited comments such as, "I have lived as an animal, now I am dying as an angel." Although compassion is not unique to Mother Teresa, and is in fact a characteristic of the redeemed and transformed life, her compassion was extraordinary and paramount to her life.

You see, your calling or glory is in you. It's not something you go get, like a degree, position, or title. It's already written in your life, though it can and must be developed. Your glory compels you to do something in every situation, a compulsion that you can choose to go with, hold back from, or ignore. It is what your heart almost always sees, knows, notices, wants to do, or is burdened by. Your glory is written on your heart, and you must go there to discover and understand it.

"You are the light of the world" (Matt. 5:14), Jesus said, and your light is not to be veiled or hidden. Shine! Let people see and experience the splendor, beauty, abundance, brilliance, and weightiness of your life so that they may have a taste of the splendor of God: "We, who with unveiled faces all reflect the Lord's glory, are being transformed into his likeness with ever-increasing glory, which comes from the Lord, who is the Spirit" (2 Cor. 3:18).

> KEEP A CLEAR EYE TOWARD LIFE'S END. DO NOT FORGET YOUR PURPOSE AND DESTINY AS GOD'S CREATURE. WHAT YOU ARE IN HIS SIGHT IS WHAT YOU ARE AND NOTHING MORE. DO NOT LET WORLDLY CARES AND ANXIETIES OR THE PRESSURES OF OFFICE BLOT OUT THE DIVINE LIFE WITHIN YOU OR THE VOICE OF GOD'S SPIRIT GUIDING YOU IN YOUR GREAT TASK OF LEADING HUMANITY TO WHOLENESS. IF YOU OPEN YOURSELF TO GOD AND HIS PLAN PRINTED DEEPLY IN YOUR HEART, GOD WILL OPEN HIMSELF TO YOU.[2]
> **—Francis of Assisi**

So, there is a brilliance, a magnificence to our lives. Scripture says that God made us a little lower than Himself and has crowned us with glory and honor (Ps. 8:4–5). And we have explored the idea that the word *glory* literally means splendor, beauty, abundance, brilliance, or weightiness—something far different from skill and proficiency. Jesus did not expend His earthly life to set men and women free to be competent. Jesus said that His mission on earth was to restore us to our original purpose: to be a display of God's glory (Isa. 61:3). Our calling is to let the world around us experience our splendor, what is abundant in us. Jobs and positions are only access points, not callings, to the people or places that God knows need our glory. When the world experiences the effect of our lives, then we are walking in our true calling.

Chapter 5

THE PATH
TO YOUR GLORY

SOMETHING HIDDEN IS ABOUT TO
BE FOUND; SOMEONE LEGENDARY IS
ABOUT TO BE DISCOVERED; SOMETHING
EXTRAORDINARY IS ABOUT TO TAKE PLACE.
—From the movie trailer for *Finding Forrester*

The good news is that we already possess a splendor and weightiness to our lives and a role to play in God's Greater Story. And there is much more to us and our part in His story than we know at this moment. But the less-welcome news is that we must take a journey in the ever-increasingness of our glory (2 Cor. 3:18). We see this journey in Scripture, modern history, and in all the great stories.

BETWEEN THE DREAMING AND THE COMING TRUE

What about Joseph? Between Joseph's dream (at age seventeen) and his ruling over all of Egypt under Pharaoh and saving multitudes from starvation (age thirty), there were thirteen years of full-on life filled with arduous work; promotions and punishments; temptations; betrayal; and false accusations by family, coworkers, and bosses. The psalmist summarized Joseph's journey in the following way:

> *[God] called for a famine on the land of Canaan,*
> *cutting off its food supply.*
> *Then he sent someone to Egypt ahead of them—*
> *Joseph, who was sold as a slave.*
> *They bruised his feet with fetters*
> *and placed his neck in an iron collar.*
> *Until the time came to fulfill his dreams,*
> *the LORD tested Joseph's character.*
> *Then Pharaoh sent for him and set him free;*
> *the ruler of the nation opened his prison door.*
> *Joseph was put in charge of all the king's household;*
> *he became ruler over all the king's possessions.*
> *He could instruct the king's aides as he pleased*
> *and teach the king's advisers. (Ps. 105:16–22*
> *NLT)*

What about Daniel? Between Daniel's being taken as a hostage into a pagan king's service (as a young man) and his later authority (in his eighties) with the king's proclamation that all people were to reverence Daniel's God, there were approximately sixty years filled with coercion, discrimination, an assassination attempt, and intense training.[1] Two passages out of the book of Daniel read:

> *God gave [to Daniel] knowledge and understanding of all kinds of literature and learning. And Daniel could understand visions and dreams of all kinds. (Dan. 1:17)*

> *The king said to Daniel, "Surely your God is the God of gods and the Lord of kings and a revealer of mysteries, for you were able to reveal this mystery."*
>
> *Then the king placed Daniel in a high position and lavished many gifts on him. He made him ruler over the entire province of Babylon and placed him in charge of all its wise men. (Dan. 2:47–48)*

What about Esther? Esther faced years of preparation, huge moral dilemmas, and life-threatening situations between the time she was taken as a mistress for a king and her opportunity to save her people from genocide. Scripture records Esther's story as: "Now the king was attracted to Esther more than to any of the other women, and *she won his favor and approval....* So he set a royal crown on her head and made her queen" (Est. 2:17). She had "come to royal position for such a time as this" (4:14). And because of Esther's cunning and courage, "for the Jews it was a time of happiness and joy, gladness and honor" (8:16).

These are but a few of the men and women mentioned in the Bible who handled the splendor, beauty, strength, and weightiness of their lives well. Scripture, in its honesty, describes many who did not, many who were destroyed by the power of their glory. Scripture is the story of God searching for those He could entrust with the real power of their lives and His kingdom without it destroying them and others: "For the eyes of the LORD range throughout the earth to strengthen those whose hearts are fully committed to him" (2 Chron. 16:9). A weak (young, untrained) heart cannot handle the true power of a person's life and its role in this epic story in which it lives. Richard Foster writes, "Power's ability to destroy human relationships is written across the face of humanity.... The demon in power is pride. True power has as its aim to set people free, whereas pride is determined to dominate."[2] How many "gifted" or "talented" people have you known or known about who overshadowed and suppressed others in their brilliance? Their very presence, though initially appreciated for what they knew or could do, eventually sidelined others, making them feel insignificant or embarrassed about their lives and roles. Though these gifted people had many admirers, they had no real friends, and the ultimate fruit of their lives was anything but sweet. It is not the gifts of the Spirit (mentioned in Romans 12 and 1 Corinthians 12) that mark a mature believer; it is the fruit of the Spirit: love, joy, peace, patience, kindness, goodness, faithfulness, gentleness, and self-control (Gal. 5:22–23).

Henrietta Mears inspired, taught, and trained some of the greatest Christian leaders of the twentieth century, including Bill Bright, who founded Campus Crusade for Christ, and Richard Halverson, chaplain of the U.S. Senate. Henrietta began one of the first Christian publishing companies, Gospel Light Press, whose influence has reached all around the world. Henrietta also founded Forest Home, a renowned retreat center in California that many would point to as facilitating a turning point in their lives. But there were years of intense hardship between all of this and her commitment at age seventeen to be whatever God wanted her to be. The backstory to her story is that the country was experiencing WWII, she was teaching in struggling rural public schools, she underwent treatment for blindness and muscular rheumatism, and she struggled with a life of singleness.[3]

We see this same idea in some of the great stories put on film such as J.R.R. Tolkien's The Lord of the Rings. In this story Sam and Frodo become more discerning, courageous, skilled, and resolute only as they keep going, approaching the fulfillment of their mission, which will save Middle Earth. Strider "the Ranger" matures into Aragorn, the heir to the throne of Gondor, and eventually rules over all of Middle Earth.

In the movie The Mask of Zorro the young protégé must develop into the man who can be the new savior of the people. He must learn how to control his anger, discern the actions of his enemies, wield his sword, and love a woman. Only then can he take on the powerful and needed role he was meant to play. In one of the classic lines in the movie, the original Zorro says, "If you are ready, we will both tempt our fates." Then pointing to his trainee's drawn sword he asks, "Do you know how to use that thing?" to which the younger replies, "The pointy end goes into the other man." Zorro mutters under his breath, "This is going to take a lot of work." It always does! The glory God has given you is not easily understood or handled. In this war of the kingdoms (the kingdom of darkness and the kingdom of light), life is not as simple as "do the best with what you've got," the equivalent of "the pointy end goes into the other man." We must become the man or woman who knows how and when to use our sword (glory).

C. S. Lewis said, "Excellence [in anything] cannot be had without experience and discipline, and therefore cannot be had by the very young."[4] Training must take place if we are to handle well the weightiness of our lives. This is not an exclusion of youth to any significant role in the transcendent story, but rather an invitation and permission to let God train you through a variety of experiences and relationships. As the older Zorro said to the developing Zorro regarding his desire to take on his enemy and fulfill what he thought was his destiny, "You would have fought bravely, but died quickly." Too many young men and women have been encouraged, urged, even coerced into activities that others saw they had ability or desire for—only to fail to some degree. What's left in these situations is usually some variation on the themes of reluctance, self-doubt, fear, or shame.

In Exodus 23:29–30, God is telling Moses that He will take him into the place He has prepared for him. But in this journey, God will not clear out all the adversaries, enemies, hindrances, and old inhabitants. God says, "Little by little I will drive them out before you, *until you have increased enough to take possession* of the land"

(v. 30). The journey must be taken if we are to increase enough to take full possession of the life and glory we have been given. It is not solely an issue of character development, but also the ability to fight spiritual opposition. The overlooked but crucial truth is that we will have to fight for every square inch of our calling. It is important that we not mistake the process of "increasing" (2 Cor. 3:18; Ex. 23:30) and "strengthening" (2 Chron. 16:9) as God's discipline, abandonment, a loss of time, or a lack of direction. It is quite the opposite. Take this process as an indication of the significance and enormity of your life and role.

As there is a journey of development, there is also a journey of discovery we must take to better understand the glory of our lives and our role in God's Greater Story. As Proverbs 4:18 says, "The *path* of the righteous is like the first gleam of dawn, shining ever brighter till the full light of day."

DECIPHERING THE MYSTERY, BREAKING THE CODE

For most of us, our pursuit of direction or purpose in life started in our late teens or early twenties. We were being asked, "What are you going to do with your life?" and, "How are you going to support yourself?" Not particularly bad questions, but not really helpful at that time. All I knew in my early twenties was that I loved gymnastics. I had competed and performed through my high school and college years, and I didn't want to leave the sport. My desire was to eventually own gymnastics centers throughout the United States.

A month before my college graduation, the director of Athletes in Action, the athletic arm of Campus Crusade for Christ, called me.

He asked what I was going to do after graduation and if I would consider joining the gymnastics ministry. This was a different direction than I wanted to go, so I explained to him that I was "called" to start gymnastics centers throughout the country to share the gospel with the students, helping fulfill the Great Commission. I used all the words I thought he wanted to hear while only meaning half of them. There was silence on the phone for a few seconds, and then he asked if he could pray for me. He did: "Father, make Gary miserable if he is not in Your will."

With that one short prayer, I was flattened. I was instantly miserable. I had no comeback except to say, "Thank you for praying for me" (a lie), and "Good-bye" (that was sincere). That misery stuck with me, as the expression goes, "like stink on manure" (apropos for my manipulative behavior). I couldn't shake it until, out of pure desperation, I told God I would join the staff of Athletes in Action, at which time the misery left and an excitement came.

My hope is that you won't write this off as another "missionary" story using guilt or shame as the hook of choice. Stay with me.

After the first year on staff, the leadership asked me to start a gymnastics center for the purpose of sharing the gospel with the students in order to "help fulfill the Great Commission in our generation." And get this—the only time I used that sentence was that fateful evening on the telephone, and I hadn't thought of it since. So, for six years I pursued my heart's desire. And at the end of that time I realized this was not my heart's deepest desire. I was not burned out—far from it. But my heart had simply moved on, desiring something deeper. Was all this a detour, a waste of time?

Not knowing at the moment, I asked God, "What was gymnastics about for me?"

What He revealed to me has guided me ever since. He showed me that gymnastics explained my glory or the weightiness of my life; it revealed to me my place in a more significant story. In response to my question, God asked me a question: "What did you enjoy about all those years of gymnastics?" My heart responded instantly, "I loved discovering what makes a great gymnastics performance and then designing the flow of elements—strength, flexibility, balance, risk, precision—to move both the judges and audience." God continued: "What about running the gymnastics center?" To my astonishment, my heart said the same thing: discovery, design, development, and fulfillment of its purpose. Gymnastics was not my heart's deepest desire, but by pursuing it I discovered what lay behind it: my *truest* desires, which revealed the glory or effect of my life. God had used gymnastics to awaken and deepen my desires.

In these early days of my "after college, on my own" life, I would have told you two things about my direction: I loved gymnastics, and I was called to Athletes in Action. Later, I would have told you I loved developing people and organizations, and I was called to Athletes in Action. Fortunately, my desires and job coincided, and I experienced joy and success. But because of this overlap and the label of "ministry" on my work, I associated calling with my job or position. So when my desires started to change—or more accurately when they deepened—I didn't know what to do with my heart's increasing disengagement from my work until I called a trusted friend who asked me three questions.

The first question he asked was, "How important are sports to you now?" My answer: "Not very." Second he asked, "How important is evangelism to you?" My answer again: "Not very." This was feeling rather embarrassing for the director of an evangelistic sports ministry. Often clarity comes only with disruption. Finally he asked, "What have you most loved doing during these recent years with AIA?" My answer: "Helping my staff find their places and do their job well." His concluding words to me were, "I think you are released from AIA." With Terry's questions and words, I was freed from a position and a place to pursue my glory and its next assignment.

There is a space in the world that is meant for you, and you alone, and awaits your glory. That place is written on your heart in the form of your desires and must be deciphered.

So, there is a process of increasing and strengthening, of discovery and development, which we must go through for the fulfillment of our calling. The glory of a person's life that is not strengthened, protected, and tempered by deep character can be more harmful than helpful. Being reluctant about the journey can cause one to dabble away his or her life, never offering true weightiness. Rather than finishing life's race with glory, what's left is just a shame.

Chapter 6

THE BATTLE OVER
YOUR CALLING

As Christians we have been taught
by Scripture and tradition to
acknowledge the spiritual dimension
as the true nucleus of reality. Human
endeavor is a related, but dependent,
outer layer. This, at any rate, is what
we say. In truth many Christians
have become practical atheists.

—George Otis, Jr.

˙mily lived fairly secure in the belief that

nd crime free. Of course there were the

˙ng toilet papered or egged, and illegal

˙o time, but no *real* crimes—no theft, assault,

˙er. So we lived like there was no evil, like there were

˙ves, no bad guys. We often left our house unlocked and even left our keys in the car. But that all changed one Saturday evening. I had just pulled our Jeep into the garage and, as usual, left the keys in it. A friend came over a few minutes later and asked where our Jeep was. Thinking she was joking or mistaken, I went out to the garage to find it empty. Someone had walked into our garage and stolen our Jeep while I was sitting only twenty feet away. It was unbelievable.

Since that day we have lived differently, like there is a thief. And far greater is the glory of our lives than even our most valued possession, and far more powerful is the Enemy of our lives than some petty criminal.

My wife and I have chosen not to live in fear, but rather with the alertness and wisdom that there are thieves who will try to take what we possess. We no longer want to live naively, but instead with an understanding of reality, eyes wide open.

THE SECRETS OF THE KINGDOM OF HEAVEN

> *"A farmer went out to sow his seed. As he was scattering the seed, some fell along the path, and the birds came and ate it up. Some fell on rocky*

places, where it did not have much soil. It sprang up quickly, because the soil was shallow. But when the sun came up, the plants were scorched, and they withered because they had no root. Other seed fell among thorns, which grew up and choked the plants. Still other seed fell on good soil, where it produced a crop—a hundred, sixty or thirty times what was sown. He who has ears, let him hear." (Matt. 13:3–9)

Then His close friends asked what His story meant. So Jesus explained,

"When anyone hears the message about the kingdom and does not understand it, the evil one comes [by force] and snatches away what was sown in his heart. This is the seed sown along the path. The one who received the seed that fell on rocky places is the man who hears the word and at once receives it with joy. But since he has no root, he lasts only a short time. When trouble [pressure] or persecution [harassment, annoyance] comes because of the word, he quickly falls away. The one who received the seed that fell among the thorns is the man who hears the word, but the worries of this life and the deceitfulness of wealth choke it, making it unfruitful." (Matt. 13:19–22)

"But the seed on good soil stands for those with
a noble and good heart, who hear the word,
retain it, and by persevering produce a crop."
(Luke 8:15)

Jesus used this story to explain to His friends the reality they were living in. The story concludes with someone gloriously flourishing, productive, and prolific because that person had a good and noble heart, heard and retained truth, and persevered. Persevered through what? And what does that have to do with retaining truth and having a noble heart? I believe Jesus' point in the story was that living this type of life, living in our glory, and finding our place in God's Greater Story is opposed. It's not simply that life is filled with hard things or that good things take effort, but that we have an Enemy.

The path to a fruitful, impressive, dynamic life is fraught with opposition ("snatches away," "falls away," "choked") … and we must live with our eyes open. To overcome this kind of opposition will take perseverance because there is a fierce and strategic assault against us; someone wants us to fail.

Too many times God gives us some revelation concerning our lives, and before we know it the understanding is gone, forgotten. Does this happen simply because we are forgetful or too busy? How could we forget something that is so important to us?

Have you ever wondered why "troubles" and "persecutions" intensify around a potential turning point in your life? Is that simply the random hardness of life? How many people do you know in midlife who, after years of experience, training, searching, and understanding, suddenly feel paralyzed and sidelined by overwhelming worries and desires—feeling like they are choking on life? Is it just that all of a sudden they became materialistic, worldly, or anal-retentive?

You don't need perseverance for an occasional battle. You need perseverance for frequent, unrelenting assaults.

Jesus started the explanation of His story by saying, "The knowledge of the secrets of the kingdom of heaven have been given to you." In other words, "This is what's really going on and how things work." That should make us sit up and pay very close attention.

In each scenario of life that Jesus presented, there were three common elements: truth (Scripture), the heart (which Jesus said was the soil), and assault. These common threads reveal what's really going on in our lives.

- God is always sowing, planting, counseling, and speaking to His people. He said, "I will instruct you and teach you in the way you should go; I will counsel you and watch over you" (Ps. 32:8).
- The heart is central—it is where your life flows from (Prov. 4:23), where the Word is planted (Ps. 119:11), where God resides (Eph. 3:17), and where the Enemy attacks.
- We have a persistent Enemy—"The thief comes only to steal [snatch away] and kill [choke] and destroy [trouble and persecution]" (John 10:10).

THE FIRST BATTLE

The first battle everyone encounters is the battle for life. There is the physical life and then there is the spiritual and soulful life.

Scripture says, "The god of this age has blinded the minds of unbelievers, so that they cannot see the light of the gospel of the glory of Christ" (2 Cor. 4:4). Everyone encounters the campaign to keep them from finding life in Christ.

I had no idea about God for the first eighteen years of my life. My parents didn't talk about Him, and we never went to church. I had no idea what happened in those buildings people referred to as churches. My sister occasionally took me to church on Christmas Eve and Easter, but all I could tell you was that a bunch of people sang to us, a man gave a speech, and a bowl was passed around for us to put money in instead of us buying tickets at the door. Then there was a time when my parents dropped me off at some church for four Sunday mornings in a row so that I could be "confirmed." The only thing that was confirmed for me was my utter confusion about this Christianity thing. I heard words like *Son of God, blood, sin, atonement, the cross, heaven and hell, righteousness,* and *resurrection,* but none of them made any sense to me. What I did understand was that if I let the pastor put some water on me, I could graduate from the class. And so the pastor sprinkled me with water, and I left, never to return. Christianity didn't make any sense to me—I was blinded to the truth.

During my freshman year in college (1973), I was sitting in my friend's apartment, watching the national news when Secretary of State Henry Kissinger announced that U.S. troops had just been put on precautionary alert because of the possible Soviet intervention in the Yom Kippur War. I had just missed the draft for the Vietnam War, so I knew that if the United States entered now, I would certainly be called up. I was not opposed to serving in the military, but two things scared me: that this would be a "world war" of epic proportions, and that if I was called upon, my life would change in undesirable ways.

Some of my friends who were Christians actually got excited and hopeful. They started talking about the "end times," the return of Jesus, and heaven. I didn't quite understand their words, but I did respect them. I wanted to understand their hope and confidence, so I went into their kitchen where they had a poster of Barbra Streisand on the wall. They had drawn a bubble from her mouth and had written the question, "Have you ever heard of the Four Spiritual Laws?" A booklet with the answer was attached to the poster. I took the booklet off the poster and read through it. At the end of the booklet was this prayer:

> *Lord Jesus, I need You. Thank You for dying on the cross for my sins. I open the door of my life and receive You as my Savior and Lord. Thank You for forgiving my sins and giving me eternal life. Take control of the throne of my life. Make me the kind of person You want me to be.*[1]

Then it asked, "Does this prayer express the desire of your heart? If it does, pray this prayer right now, and Christ will come into your life, as He promised."

I did, right then and there. And it all made sense to me. My eyes were open, and I could "see the light of the glorious gospel of Christ" for the first time. I had won the first battle and found life.

THE SECOND BATTLE

If the Enemy is unsuccessful in stopping the seed of the kingdom of God from being planted in your heart with new life, then he will try to stop the seed from growing into its intended stature (an "[oak] of righteousness, a planting of the LORD for the display of his splendor" [Isa. 61:3]) and from multiplying ("yielded a crop, a hundred times more than was sown" [Luke 8:8]). Understand that the battle intensifies now because we are aware of it.

As I have examined my own life, the lives of others, and Scripture, I have found a pattern to the Enemy's attack—he uses distance, diminishment, disdain, and disqualification to render us useless in the kingdom of God.

The first wave of attack is to distance us from our hearts and desires through pain or wounding. If distance is unsuccessful or unsustained, the next assault is to diminish the glory of our lives to the point where we don't want to offer it. If diminishment doesn't work, the third strike is to cause us to disdain our glory through the power of shame. Finally, if all else fails, the Enemy launches the accusation of disqualification. The battle is never easy, but we can fight wisely when we recognize and understand the Enemy's strategy.

Distance

Many people I talk with admit that they are unaware of any passion, any strong desire that is good and central to their being—and they often confess that nothing seems to "move" them. It is simply not true.

As film director, producer, and writer John Boorman wrote, "What is passion? It is surely the becoming of a person.... The more extreme and the more expressed that passion is, the more unbearable does life seem without it. It reminds us that if passion dies or is denied, we are partly dead and that soon, come what may, we will be wholly so."[2]

We are by our very nature creatures of purpose and passion. As we've seen that Scripture says, "It is God who is producing in you both the desire and the ability to do what pleases him" (Phil. 2:13 ISV). God has placed in your heart certain desires that define who you are and what you were created to do. These desires are core, historic, and indelible.

So why are our deepest desires so hard to find? Distance. Something has caused us to keep our distance from our truest desires by making them feel unsafe or untrue. If you go back into a person's story, you can usually find their deepest desires and the assault against those desires—the words and actions that made those desires seem useless, foolish, or dangerous.

Weren't some of those wounding words and actions the result of our misunderstandings, misperceptions, or misinterpretations of intent? Yes, some were. Weren't some of those incidents random acts of violence as a result of living in a fallen world? Yes, again, some were. But do you believe everything that happens to you is by chance or happenstance, random or unintentional? Some are, but that leaves room for some that aren't.

Remember Jesus' explanation of the secrets of the kingdom of heaven and His statement that He came to bring life, but that there is a thief who is here to steal, kill, and destroy that life? Satan's intention is to distance or deaden us from our deepest desires that were meant to help guide us to our place in this world.

Satan is a master deceiver, constantly reinterpreting words, actions, looks, situations, and feelings. Jesus said that Satan "was a murderer from the beginning, not holding to the truth, for there is no truth in him. When he lies, he speaks his native language, for he is a liar and the father of lies" (John 8:44). Satan usually, very quickly, offers an "understanding" or interpretation of a situation with the intent to distance you from what is truest about you. His lies are always at the level of the heart because "your heart ... determines the course of your life" (Prov. 4:23 NLT). Let me give you some examples from my own life.

Seventh grade. My homeroom study hour. My teacher stepped out of the room for a moment, and as she did several boys across the room started throwing art-crayons at the boy next to me. He was scared to death. In the moment, indignation and courage welled up in me at what was taking place. I warned the bullies that they'd better stop, but my warning only diverted their anger and attack toward me. As they continued their attack, I called the leader of their group to the middle of the room. With his chest pushed out and hands gesturing for me to take a swing, I knew that the only way this would stop was to take him on. Remembering how Bond, James Bond, handled situations like this, I knew that one punch to the face would end it all. So I hauled off and hit him, but he didn't go down. Instead, he took a few steps back and then lunged forward and put me in a headlock. I found myself on my knees unable to breathe, hearing the other kids pleading for him to let me go. The room faded to black, and the next thing I knew, I was on my back looking at the ceiling. I got back up to the jeers and laughter of the hoodlums and returned to my seat before the teacher came back to the room. I had stepped up to do something good, to offer my help, to intervene … and I was humiliated. My strength was not enough. The sentence that lodged itself in my young heart, though unknown to me at that moment, was, "Don't try to help people; mind your own business; do what is expected of you and nothing more." From that day forward, I took a few steps back from my heart and its desires.

In another situation, our college gymnastics team went to the qualifying competition for the national championship. The first day of competition, I felt a little "off"—not as fine-tuned as I had trained to be. I was a little foggy, my timing was slightly off, and my body was aching for some reason. The next day, I noticed bumps on my skin. I went to the athletic trainer to ask him about these strange bubbles on my body, and he immediately quarantined me for the rest of the competition. I had chicken pox! I was twenty years old, and I had been training for years for this competition—and I was taken out by a childhood illness, something I should have been immune to. In my search for understanding I quickly "heard" the words: "This is the way life goes; what you want and what you work for will be taken away." So I took a few more steps away from my heart and its desires, and I became more cautious and calculating.

During my work with Athletes in Action, we started a gymnastics center in Southern California where we could train both ourselves and young men and women to compete, perform, and share the gospel around the world. One afternoon when the men's team was practicing before the kids came in for their gymnastics lesson, one of the men asked me to spot him while he was doing his dismount from the parallel bars. The dismount was a double-back somersault that he had done many times before. He had a crash pad to land on, but he wanted me to be there, just in case. As he swung down from a handstand, his knees rose above his head, and he let go of the parallel bars. He grabbed his legs, pulling into a tight tuck to increase his rotation, and at that moment I knew he was not going to make it to his feet. So I stepped in and bumped his hips to increase his rotation ... and he rolled out of my hands, landing upside down on his neck. Hitting the crash pad, he recoiled upon impact and then collapsed, paralyzed from the neck down. This event was so tragic and overwhelming that I could not and would not work through what happened until God (twenty-seven years later) forced me to. The deep belief and fear that I had done this to him, that it was my fault he was paralyzed, led me to the belief that I could tragically hurt other people who asked for my help. This caused me to greatly increase the distance between me and my heart's desires.

These kinds of experiences cause us to get very nervous or even terrified when we get close to our heart's desires. In particular situations we find ourselves either unable to engage (like going quiet or staying shallow or looking for the exit door), or doing things that we wish we hadn't (like being loud, dominating, constantly joking or bantering), or becoming angry, on edge, and irritated for no apparent reason.

Look, the Enemy doesn't have to kill us to prevent us from becoming a display of God's splendor. He just has to distance us from our hearts and desires so that we become disoriented, disabled, deactivated, and disconnected. This distancing happens slowly, incrementally over time until we are so far from our heart that we don't even know it exists. That's why, "Guard your heart above all else, for it determines the course of your life" (Prov. 4:23 NLT).

God has told us to be careful not to become enslaved to anything: "It is for freedom that Christ has set us free. Stand firm, then, and do not let yourselves be burdened again by a yoke of slavery" (Gal. 5:1). These kinds of lies and deceptions create a collar of slavery that leads us in directions we don't want to go—attempting, and often succeeding, to define who we are. How many times have we asked ourselves, "Why do I keep doing that?" or "Why can't I get myself to _____?" These questions are an indication of a "yoke of slavery"—the kind Christ has come to free us from.

When the avoidance of pain (being overlooked or ignored, rejected or excluded, ridiculed or misunderstood) or the drive to meet a need (to be validated, significant, applauded, seen, and heard) dictate our words and action, we are enslaved. Scripture says, "A man is a slave to whatever has mastered him" (2 Peter 2:19).

I have met many men and women who have something weighty and beautiful to offer. It's on the tip of their tongue or fingertips, but they can't offer it because of a fear that was created years or decades earlier, largely unknown to them but nonetheless present and controlling. We label and excuse this person as shy or not having much to offer. I have also met many who, through their words and actions, are asking for or demanding acceptance and validation in exchange for their offering. We label these people as controlling, draining, or high maintenance. Both types are people who possess a splendor, abundance, beauty, and weightiness … but that splendor has been infected or contaminated by the presumed failures or pain in their lives.

I hope you understand that recognizing these wounds and defining these false-self influencers did not come to me quickly or all at one time. The understanding of these yokes of slavery and the way they have affected my life surfaced during prayer, while hearing another person's story, in counseling, during times of self-evaluation, and through conversations with friends. And I can assure you there are other "yokes of slavery" that God will reveal to me throughout my life.

It is also important to know that even though I have dealt with the yokes I've mentioned, I still hear and feel their presence, though now from more of a distance. It's like sleeping in a mosquito-infested area under netting. After you kill the couple of mosquitoes that somehow found their way to the inside of your canopy and were biting you, you still hear the buzzing of other mosquitoes outside, looking for an opening. Their "voice" persists, but their presence is no longer internal and therefore does not have to define or direct your life.

Diminishment

As we begin to discover (or more accurately rediscover) our heart's desires and embrace them, the attack will likely turn to the diminishment (self-diminishment) of your glory. The Enemy's intention is to get you to view your weightiness as less than it is and therefore convince you not to offer it. *Diminishment* is more in the moment or "in your face," while *distancing* is more historic and from a deeper place. *Diminishment* is more often heard, while *distancing* is more likely to be felt. The assault of diminishment often comes at us in the form of accusation.

While taking a brief break during a fairly intense meeting over a human-resource issue, I "heard" a very clear voice say to me, "They don't care what you think; just keep quiet and leave as soon as can." I didn't actually hear a voice but rather a thought. It was so coherent that I looked around to see if someone had spoken to me, but there was no one in the room; I was alone. My first reaction was to agree with the accusation and then I realized how "out of context" this thought was. This wasn't my evaluating or processing; this was a very direct, pointed "statement" or accusation, and its intention was to shut me down.

God has told us that Satan is not only the father of lies (John 8:44), but the accuser of believers (Rev. 12:10). Satan is very good at his trade. Diminishment through accusation is as effective as distancing through wounding. What makes Satan's accusations so potent is that they come to us as an internal voice, and this voice mimics our own. We then entertain the accusation and accept it as our own internal reasoning and perception.

During one of my calling retreats, I asked the audience about the accusations they commonly hear. With raised hands, they were reporting internal statements like:

It's too late.

You don't know what you're talking about.

You really have nothing to offer.

You're a joke.

You'll only make things worse.

Diminishing accusations like these can be crippling if they are accepted and agreed with.

Oswald Chambers said that the test as to the validity of a thought is to see what the outcome would be by pushing the thought to its logical conclusion. If that conclusion would be "something that God would condemn, allow it no more way."[3] This is great wisdom and can be very helpful.

Countless times, as I looked at faces in the audience while speaking, I would hear something like, *See, you are boring them.... You make no sense.... You are disappointing them.* If I went with that thought, I would start second-guessing myself, becoming intimidated and apologetic, and I would rush to finish and get out of the room.

Another helpful question is, "Where is this thought coming from?" Often, as I ask myself this question, I realize how out of context, how foreign these diminishing thoughts really are—that they are not my thoughts.

Accusations, at their core, are judgments or verdicts. Paul said, "Do not pass judgment ... even on yourself" (1 Cor. 4:3–5, author's paraphrase). Satan tries to get you to judge your glory, to diminish it so that you will not offer it. Don't do it. Resist. Paul goes on to say, "Therefore judge nothing before the appointed time; wait till the Lord comes. He will bring to light what is hidden in darkness and will expose the motives of men's hearts. At that time each will receive *his praise* from God" (v. 5).

We must be vigilant in defending ourselves against this attack. We must not entertain or accept these diminishing "internal statements."

We must rescind, annul, renounce, and break the agreements we have made over the years that have developed into defining statements in our lives.

Let me describe two categories of accusation that may be less apparent, but very common and effective.

Comparison

It's one of the oldest tactics in the book, and yet we are surprised and ensnared by it every time. We experience another person's glory, and the Enemy is right there whispering something like, "That's amazing, isn't it? People don't respond to you like they do to him/her. You will never be anything like that person. You are such a lightweight, an amateur, a cheap imitation—that's why no one is asking you to speak/pray/teach/meet/write/work like they do that person."

We can disarm this accusation, not by minimizing the other person, but by realizing that another's glory never diminishes our own. Every person's glory is needed. Every person's glory has its own function and place. Every person's glory is developing.

I remember how vulnerable I was to this regarding God's charge to write this book. My book agent told me that what I had written was awful and that he wouldn't represent my work to any publisher. And as if that wasn't hard enough, one of my closest friends and colleagues was pursued by publishers to write even more books. The accusations were flying: *Your writing a book is a joke; why do you think no one wants to publish you? You'll never be a writer like John; don't keep fooling yourself—stop writing.* Now I realize some seven years later, this book had its own time that was connected with my journey and was different from John's.

Another "comparison" tactic that I have observed is less recognized. It is the comparison to someone not with "greater gifting" but rather "without gifting" in the particular thing they put forth. It's the singer or musician who has everyone on edge because they are trying so hard but succeeding so little. It's the speaker or teacher who is trying to be funny or profound and obviously isn't. It's the person offering counsel to another and being completely unhelpful. It's the person who says he or she is a leader or team builder … and yet you wouldn't want to have lunch with them. It is here that the accusation comes: *That's what you're like when you offer your so-called gifting; it's embarrassing, isn't it? You're just like that.* And so, out of disgust, you stop offering your glory.

So either out of intimidation or embarrassment, you have been "talked into" diminishing your glory to the point where you do not want to offer it.

> *Make a careful exploration of who you are and the work you have been given, and then sink yourself into that. Don't be impressed with yourself. Don't compare yourself with others. Each of you must take responsibility for doing the creative best you can with your own life.* (Gal. 6:4–5 MSG)

Relative Value

Many people I've talked to are immobilized by the perception, which started as an accusation, that if God wanted them to offer their glory, they would get paid to do it full-time; those with weighty gifting are recognized for it and therefore given pay, position, and platform.

Permit me to briefly debunk this malicious idea. First, as we've discussed before, there is no position, paid or unpaid, that can fully encompass or accommodate the glory of your life—it cannot be restricted to job description. Second, there is no person (or organization) on this earth that controls your ability to walk in your calling—not a person of wealth, authority, stature, or connection. Third, impact is not exclusive to or guaranteed by working in ministry (a church or nonprofit, philanthropic, or mission organization). I have known many who had to leave a ministry to find their ministry.

Disdain

Even if we refuse to be distanced from our hearts and its desires or to accept the diminishing accusations of the Enemy, the Enemy will still try to take us out by getting us to disdain the glory that we have begun to see and own.

You can hear the disdain in statements like, "I wish I didn't see the way I see or hear the way I hear," or "I wish God would stop asking me to speak up or asking me to *do* something." This is the germination of disliking and disowning our splendor.

David writes in Psalm 4:2, "How long, O men, will you turn my glory into shame?" Isn't it true that we could all write this from our life experience?

During a counseling session, I had a revelation that brought me great clarity about my life. I said to my counselor, "Let me explain to you what goes on in my head all the time—I am constantly trying to assess the purpose of something and what may get in its way or undermine it." And as I said this I remembered how, if I could pick another life, I would like to have been a Secret Service agent or a surgeon—someone whose goal is to find the threat and eliminate it so that life may go on and flourish. These weren't simply boyhood and young-adulthood fantasies; these dreams described something of my design, my function, and what I was made to do.

Over the last several years, I have been criticized for being "negative," "a hindrance," and "a wet blanket." During a staff meeting a number of years ago, I brought up a suggestion for consideration related to an idea we were discussing. One of my colleagues said to everyone in response to my suggestion, "Have you noticed how Gary is just like Mr. MacPhee in C. S. Lewis's book *That Hideous Strength?*" I wasn't familiar with the story or character, but I could tell by his expression and tone that he was shaming me; sometimes you just know.

Have there been moments when I have been nothing more than negative and argumentative? Yes, much to my sorrow. And have there been times when I have had something to say that was needed and helpful, but I said it in an unhelpful, wrong way? Yes. But there are also many times when I have brought up something that I "saw," and it proved to be exactly what was needed. So often in these moments there has been ridicule from another because they felt threatened and didn't want their idea restrained—even for the sake of its refinement and success—so they found it necessary to belittle what I had to offer.

Because of scenarios like this, I have felt driven to the point of asking God, not for the honing of my calling or for perseverance, but rather to take this part of my calling away. I had come to disdain it because offering it caused too much pain.

Can you recognize your story in mine—you stepped out to offer your strength, beauty, and abundance, and consequently you have gotten hurt? It's not so much the difficulty or unpredictability that these moments bring; it's the accompanying tormenting message. Messages like, "It's not worth it," or "This is what makes people not want to be around you," or "You do more harm than good" ... and so, sadly, we are driven in the opposite direction and walk away from those things that make us who we are.

Disqualification

Now, if all of this attack and assault does not stop us from offering our glory to others, then the Enemy plays his wild card—disqualification. He whispers in our ear, *I know what you did; you blew it; you're a disgrace; it's too late for you; you crossed the line; it's over.* Those types of accusations combined with the sensitivity of our hearts to sin and disobedience are enough to shut us down. If we are not immersed in the truths of Scripture, we will easily and wholeheartedly buy in to this lie.

Satan understands the gravity of sin. He's experienced the consequences himself, and he instigated it with humanity. He knows how the "Deep Magic" works, as the White Witch called the issue of sin in *The Lion, the Witch and the Wardrobe*. Sin has consequences—"sin will take you further than you want to go, it will keep you longer than you want to stay, and it will cost you more than you want to pay."[4] Satan uses the conviction of sin with believers because he is confident it will sideline them. The White Witch said, "Every traitor belongs to me as my lawful prey and that for treachery I have a right to a kill.... [T]hat human creature is mine. His life is forfeit to me. His blood is my property."[5] But there is a "magic deeper still" that Aslan speaks of—"when a willing victim who had committed no treachery was killed in a traitor's stead ... Death itself would start working backward."[6] This is the truth of 1 John 2:2: "the atoning sacrifice [of Jesus Christ] for our sins." It is this "magic deeper still" that we must use against this assault of disqualification.

> *If we claim to be without sin, we deceive ourselves and the truth is not in us. If we confess our sins, he is faithful and just and will forgive us our sins and purify us from all unrighteousness. (1 John 1:8–9)*

> *There is now no condemnation for those who are in Christ Jesus, because through Christ Jesus the law of the Spirit of life has set me free from the law of sin and death. (Rom. 8:1–2)*

> *God's gifts and his call are irrevocable. (Rom. 11:29)*

> *For no matter how many promises God has made, they are "Yes" in Christ. (2 Cor. 1:20)*

The weapons we fight with are not the weapons of the world. On the contrary, they have divine power to demolish strongholds. We demolish arguments and every pretension that sets itself up against the knowledge of God, and we take captive every thought to make it obedient to Christ. (2 Cor. 10:4–5)

When we sin, our solution is still Jesus Christ—all that was accomplished for us through His death, resurrection, and ascension. Let sin drive us back to God's love, sacrifice, and mercy—and His pursuit of us. Let it cause us to remember, once again, our unequivocal need for Him—for forgiveness, deliverance, life, and freedom. And let this remembrance increase our love for Jesus Christ (He who is forgiven much, loves much [Luke 7:47]) and our conviction to live as a display of God's splendor (Isa. 61:2–3).

GUARDING OUR HEARTS

Understanding the assaults against our calling is very helpful, but it does not set us free. Understanding is not healing; clarity is not restoration. You can understand that you have a laceration, but that doesn't stop the bleeding. You can have clarity as to the type of prison you are in and why, but you are still locked up. Understanding and clarity allow us to be on the defense. But the intervention and healing of God allows us to be on the offense.

So how do we handle these assaults against our hearts and calling, especially those from the past?

Exposure

First, ask God to shine His light on your life to expose:

- the defining assaults that have distanced you from your desires
- the agreements you have made with diminishment
- the times you have disdained your glory
- any sin not dealt with that the Enemy continues to use against you

> *Everything exposed by the light becomes visible, for it is light that makes everything visible. (Eph. 5:13–14)*

> *"If you are filled with light, with no dark corners, then your whole life will be radiant, as though a floodlight were filling you with light." (Luke 11:36 NLT)*

Asking God to shine His light on these circumstances is most effective either in a time of solitude and silence or with a few others who understand and are focused on your heart and glory.

When God reveals something, ask Him to show you the reality of the event:

- what really happened versus how you perceived it
- the lie about you, God, and others, or the lie about how life works that was embedded in your heart

- the false self/inauthentic behavior that you have embraced

I have found it extremely important during these times with God to journal what I hear in response to these questions. It is better not to rely on your memory alone.

Confession

Confess the lies that you have believed and allowed to define your life rather than your Creator's truth. Renounce the lies and announce the truth (Scripture): "We demolish arguments and every pretension that sets itself up against the knowledge of God, and we take captive every thought to make it obedient to Christ" (2 Cor. 10:5).

Repentance

The truest form of repentance is not only stopping the behavior that you are repenting of, but intentionally doing the actions that were being blocked—do the opposite.

If God were to reveal to you that you play it safe by controlling things (dominating conversations and decision making/ direction setting, "leading," "keeping things moving," being assertive), then stop offering your input all the time. Let others offer instead.

Or if God reveals that you play it safe by staying silent, being reserved ("mostly listening," "letting others speak up," "staying in a posture of humility"), then allow your voice to come forth. Start speaking up.

This is true repentance.

Jesus tells us that when we intend to live a glorious and fruitful life, we will face opposition. Overcoming this kind of opposition will take perseverance because of the fierceness and longevity of the assault against us … and it will be fought at the level of the heart (Prov. 4:23).

The Adversary has been trying to distance you from your heart and desires (which are your means of guidance) throughout your life primarily through deep wounding. And if those wounds are not dealt with, they will successfully produce a yoke of slavery (Gal. 5:1). The good news is that Jesus came to heal our wounded heart and set us free (Isa. 61:1–3). But His intention and our understanding of this must be joined with cooperation in the process.

Once we start down the path of the recognition, healing, and restoration of our hearts and desires, the Enemy will turn his tactics to the diminishment of our glory. He will bombard us with accusations of insignificance, disinterest, futility, or guile with the intent to get us not to offer our glory. And these internal diminishing statements, if accepted, will turn into judgments against God's glory in us.

As we recognize and embrace our glory and refuse the internal diminishing accusations against it, the Adversary will then try to get us to disdain our calling through shame. This often happens when the offering of our glory is ridiculed or rejected, and the Enemy floods us with shame to the point where we resent our calling. If shame is allowed to take root, we will disown and walk away from our glory.

Finally, if all else fails, the Enemy will use disqualification, accusing us of "crossing the line" with God and therefore losing our place in His Greater Story. When we sin, our solution is still Jesus

Christ—all that was accomplished for us through His death, resurrection, and ascension. We allow our sin to drive us back to God's love, sacrifice, mercy, and pursuit of us with an assurance that "God's gifts and his call are irrevocable" (Rom. 11:29).

Here are some Scriptures full of truths to announce over the renunciation of the lies:

I am God's child. (John 1:12)

I am a branch of Jesus Christ, the True Vine, and a channel of His life. (John 15:5)

As a disciple, I am a friend of Jesus Christ. (John 15:15)

I have been chosen and appointed to bear fruit. (John 15:16)

I have been justified. (Rom. 5:1)

I am free from condemnation. (Rom. 8:1–2)

I am assured that God works for my good in all circumstances. (Rom. 8:28)

I am free from any condemnation brought against me, and I cannot be separated from the love of God. (Rom. 8:31–39)

I am united with the Lord, and I am one with Him in spirit. (1 Cor. 6:17)

I am God's temple. (1 Cor. 3:16)

I have been bought with a price, and I belong to God. (1 Cor. 6:19–20)

I am a member of Christ's body. (1 Cor. 12:27)

I have been established, anointed, and sealed by God. (2 Cor. 1:21–22)

I am a minister of reconciliation for God. (2 Cor. 5:17–21)

I have been chosen by God and adopted as His child. (Eph. 1:3–8)

I am seated with Jesus Christ in the heavenly realm. (Eph. 2:6)

I am God's workmanship. (Eph. 2:10)

I may approach God with freedom and confidence. (Eph. 3:12)

I am confident that God will complete the good work He started in me. (Phil. 1:6)

I am a citizen of heaven. (Phil. 3:20)

I can do all things through Christ, who strengthens me. (Phil. 4:13)

I have been redeemed and forgiven of all my sins. (Col. 1:13–14)

I am complete in Christ. (Col. 2:9–10)

I am hidden with Christ in God. (Col. 3:1–4)

I have not been given a spirit of fear but of power, love, and a sound mind. (2 Tim. 1:7)

I have direct access to the throne of grace through Jesus Christ. (Heb. 4:14–16)

I am born of God and the Evil One cannot touch me. (1 John 5:18)[7]

Chapter 7

AWAKENING YOUR DESIRES

THE SECRET OF A GREAT LIFE IS OFTEN A MAN'S
SUCCESS IN DECIPHERING THE MYSTERIOUS SYMBOLS
VOUCHSAFED TO HIM, UNDERSTANDING THEM
AND SO LEARNING TO WALK IN THE TRUE PATH.
—Aleksandr Solzhenitsyn

Bruce screams out to God in desperation, "Tell me what's going on, what should I do—give me a signal!" Before he can take another breath, he passes a brightly lit sign: *Caution Ahead*. So distracted and blinded by his own lostness and anger, he misses the message. Again he cries out, "I need Your guidance, Lord; please send me a sign!" Immediately a large road-crew truck pulls in front of him. The back of the truck is filled with street signs in plain view: *Stop. Dead End. Wrong Way. Do Not Enter.* Oblivious to any connection or significance these signs have to his prayer, Bruce speeds past the truck and into catastrophe. This scene from the movie *Bruce Almighty* is a perfect illustration of how most of us deal with the search for our glory. The answer is closer than we have been led to believe.

God has given us a road map for the life each of us is meant to live. But the map is contained in a place we seldom go—our hearts— and it is written in "cryptic form" and "mysterious symbols," symbols that we seldom try to decipher. In frustration, irritation, and anger we bypass our hearts and desires and "despair because our lives seem meaningless."[1]

DECIPHERING THE CODE

David, one of the most glorious human characters in Scripture, named among history's handful "who through faith conquered king- doms, administered justice, and gained what was promised; who shut the mouths of lions, quenched the fury of the flames, and escaped the edge of the sword; whose weakness was turned to strength; and who became powerful in battle and routed foreign armies" (Heb. 11:33–34), described his life as one of living out his heart's desire: "You [God] have granted [me] the desire of [my] heart and have not withheld the request of [my] lips" (Ps. 21:2). David walked with

God and pursued the desires of his heart. That was his internal reality. From an external perspective "David had served God's purpose in his own generation" (Acts 13:36).

David understood the role of discipline, wisdom, skill, long-term strategy, prayer, and obedience to God; but the living out of his purpose, calling, and glory was found in his desires. He writes, "Delight yourself in the LORD and he will give you the desires of your heart" (Ps. 37:4). David's expression, *the desires of your heart,* literally means "that which the deepest, truest part of you continually seeks or prays for." There are certain core desires and longings that you have not been able to escape. These longings have been with you for as long as you can remember, surfaced by particular events, stories, or conversations throughout your life. You may have ignored them as illegitimate, dismissed them as unimportant, or misunderstood them, but like a true friend and ally, they have stayed with you. You would be lost without them.

While Psalm 37:4 is a familiar verse, it has of recent been misinterpreted in regards to its true meaning. Most commonly many people have understood the meaning of the verse as being "disregard all of your desires and work on loving God more because all of your other desires or longings compete with or diminish your ability to love God." And, in this interpretation, when and if you love God *enough,* He will give you one or two desires of your heart, and these are really more His desires for you, not your desires for yourself.

Having been in vocational ministry my entire working life, I have seen men and women trying to love God wholeheartedly while shutting down their hearts by dismissing their desires. It never seems to work. How many unhappy, unfulfilled, dispassionate Christians struggling to love God have you encountered? The majority of their energy seems to be spent fighting personal sin and disappointment with a faltering sense of discipline and commitment. So many have made their pursuit of God solely a matter of their "will," believing that desire is the enemy of intimacy with God. Encountering repeated failure, they work harder on strengthening their resolve and silencing the passions of their heart. But as Oswald Chamber says, "When we speak of a man having a weak will, we mean he is without any impelling passion, he is the creature of every dominating influence; with good people he is good, with bad people he is bad, not because he is a hypocrite, but because he has no ruling passion."[2] Desire or passion is not a deterrent to our walking with God and discovering our calling; it is the *means* to both.

A friend of mine went to a counselor as he realized that he had lived most of his adult life without passion and joy, even while holding "good" jobs and providing nice things for his family. He was tired of who he had become and so was his wife. One of the most liberating things the counselor said to him was, "You don't have to live continually depressed and angry." He had driven his desires underground, deadening his heart, and found himself directionless, angry, compromised, weak, and pervasively unhappy even though his life appeared well ordered and well lived. He had no ruling passion, becoming vulnerable to every persuasive force, and delighting in God or anything else, for that matter, seemed artificial.

In *The Screwtape Letters*, C. S. Lewis uses fiction to teach on the strategies used by the kingdom of darkness against humanity. In this story a senior demon (Screwtape) teaches his protégé (Wormwood) how to disrupt the advancement of the kingdom of God by keeping humans away from their calling. At one point Screwtape gives Wormwood a direct order: "Your job, Wormwood, is to provide me with people who do not care." And such has been the work of the kingdom of darkness against Christians. Unwittingly, in the desire to "love and serve God," many have lived according to the idea that if you abandon or deaden all other desires, your love for God will become exclusive and pure. And so a woman walks away from her love to sculpt beauty through gardening and interior decorating, because there is no time in this world's condition for such frivolities, and then she wonders why her heart seems so dull toward God. A man shuts down his inclination toward and enjoyment of assessing how to make something better, because he was told he just creates more work for everyone, slows things down, and doesn't know how to be content. So he walks with unspoken shame over the fact that he feels closer to God in his workshop than in church, his quiet times, or ministry activity. You see, the heart is a delicate thing. Like the ecosystem, you cannot eliminate one element without affecting another. How can you "love the Lord your God with all your heart" (Mark 12:30) if you have lost it through neglect and starvation?

Speaking to those who had replaced an authentic love for God with religious pretense, Jesus said, "For this people's heart has become calloused; they hardly hear with their ears, and they have closed their eyes" (Matt. 13:15). And so for most of us, we have lived more like Bruce Nolan in *Bruce Almighty,* having eyes but not able to see what's right in front of us.

LIVING IN THE "AND"

We must live in the "and" of "delight yourself in the LORD *and* he will give you the desires of your heart," staying present to our desires in our pursuit of God. In the story of Eric Liddell, portrayed in the movie *Chariots of Fire*, Eric's sister challenges him to get serious with God and his calling to China by forgetting his Olympic desires and opportunity. She is concerned that Eric is neglecting his faith because he is "so full of running." Eric comments to Jenny, "I believe that God made me for a purpose for China. He also made me fast, and when I run I feel His pleasure…. To give it up would be to hold Him in contempt…. To win is to honor Him." Could that be true—that to give up our greatest desires would be disrespectful to our Creator and to live them out would be honoring? Perhaps this is what the apostle meant when he wrote, "To this end also we pray for you always, that our God will count you worthy of your calling, and *fulfill every desire [delight, pleasure, satisfaction] for goodness and the work of faith with power*" (2 Thess. 1:11 NASB). Eric, "The Flying Scotsman," won a gold medal and set a world record in the 1924 Paris Olympics before going to China. Eric was a man who walked with God and followed his heart, as my friend and ally Bart paraphrases Psalm 37:4. The realization of your calling is the fulfillment of your truest desires.

Really, any desire? Are all desires good?

> *Don't love the world's goods. Love of the world squeezes out love for the Father. Practically everything that goes on in the world—wanting your own way, wanting everything for yourself,*

*wanting to appear important—has nothing
to do with the Father. It just isolates you from
him. (1 John 2:15–16 MSG)*

DESIRE REQUIRES MATURITY

The path into our calling has two tracks: one of discovery (of our glory) and the other of development (into strength and maturity). Both must be traveled simultaneously, for the journey into desire will require increasing maturity; the higher the level of realization of calling, the higher the level of cunning that is required. "The naive believes everything," David says, "but the sensible [prudent, shrewd] man considers [perceives, discerns, distinguishes] his steps" (Prov. 14:15 NASB). When we were children, we thought like children: We took things at face value, and we reacted immediately because the present was all we knew. But as we grew older, we realized that things are not always as they seem. We didn't realize in our youth that there is a lot at play in life, both in ourselves and in the world. Paul, who described people walking in their callings as "fulfill[ing] every desire for goodness" (2 Thess. 1:11 NASB), also wrote, "Examine everything carefully; hold fast to that which is good" (1 Thess. 5:21 NASB). Jesus warned that not everyone who does amazing things for God is of God. His counsel was to test actions or words and look at what people produce: "You will know them by their fruits" (Matt. 7:16 NASB).

I remember a time when one of my kids wanted to eat a taco left over from dinner. This would have been all right, except that it had been sitting out for several hours. The taco looked fine, but I knew that it was not as it seemed. There was probably invisible-to-the-naked-eye bacteria on it, and the end result of the desire to eat that taco would not be good. My son was dealing with his desire as a child; I was handling it as an adult. Paul said that when we are young we think as a child, but when we hit adulthood we must think differently; we should see things more fully (1 Cor. 13:11).

THREE SOURCES OF DESIRES

Not every desire is good. Whether a desire is good or bad depends on where that desire comes from. There are the desires of our sinful nature, which Paul says are obvious because of their fruit:

> *When you follow the desires of your sinful nature, the results are very clear: sexual immorality, impurity, lustful pleasures, idolatry, sorcery, hostility, quarreling, jealousy, outbursts of anger, selfish ambition, dissension, division, envy, drunkenness, wild parties, and other sins like these. (Gal. 5:19–21 NLT)*

These desires are aligned with the desires of the world. These worldly desires have wreaked havoc on individual lives, marriages, churches, communities, companies, cultures, etc., and because of this, the church has distanced itself from desire altogether.

Scripture says that "each one is tempted when, by his own evil desire, he is dragged away and enticed" (James 1:14). Another source of desire is the demonic realm. Have you ever had an all-of-the-sudden, out-of-context strong desire? Sure you have. Urges like pornography, leaving your marriage, getting drunk, quitting, committing suicide, or hitting someone. At that moment the desire feels so real, but many times, when you stop to really think about it, it is completely irrational. There is a story in the New Testament of a couple who had sold some land, intending to give the proceeds to the apostles for the church (Acts 5:1–11). Scripture says that Satan influenced their hearts so that they secretly kept part of the proceeds, declaring to have given it all. In other words, Satan introduced a desire in their hearts that they followed, and the results weren't good. Years ago, while traveling to speak to a group in another state, I had an overwhelming desire to look at pornography. I had not seen anything to trigger this idea. The desire was out of the blue and relentless. After a long period of battling with this unholy desire, trying to silence it without success, I realized that this was not from me. When I turned from resisting my heart to resisting the Adversary, the desire left. It was a diversionary tactic from the Enemy to dull my heart, both to God and to my calling.

An even subtler source of desire comes from the deep hurts or wounds we have received over our lives. Every wound we incur verbally, physically, or circumstantially creates a desire and strategy for avoidance. These desires are the most difficult to differentiate from our truest desires because they reside in a deep place, they feel like the truest part of us, and they are triggered by so many things. A part of me is very cynical about life, scrutinizing everything and everyone, holding back my trust and engagement. I found several of the headwaters to this polluted, treacherous river in my soul.

From one of my earliest memories, my dad bought me the Rifleman's toy replica rifle. This was one of the most prized and anticipated gifts I had ever been given as a boy. This gun allowed me to be the Rifleman, Chuck Connors, whom I idealized every week through the TV series, as he loved his family and fiercely and skillfully fought bad guys. After several days of playing with the toy gun in my home, I took it over to a neighbor friend's house. He asked me if he could hold it after admiring it in my hands. When I handed it over to him, he swung the gun at a tree trunk and broke it in two. My dad did nothing—neither scolding the neighborhood boy nor getting me a new one. It was taken from me forever. This may sound trivial to you, but not to me as a young boy. Something shifted in me that day, and a desire formed: to be safe from the unsafe. So part of my desire to analyze things as to their trueness, sincerity, or genuineness is not good, especially when the fruit is being untrusting and disengaged with others. But there is an aspect of this part of me that is also a part of my glory. We will go into this much deeper in the next chapter.

There's also the source of your truest, God-created desires that clearly reveals your glory … and the source is your heart. I need to clarify what I mean by *heart*. I'm not referring to the modern understanding of "feelings"—as in the head (thinking) and the heart (feeling); that is a Greek view of the heart, which is how most of us were educated and thus how we interpreted the word. I am referring instead to the Hebrew understanding of the word as used in Scripture: the truest, deepest part of you—your soul. That part from which you must believe (Rom. 10:9); from which you must forgive (Matt. 18:35); from which you are to work (Col. 3:23); from which you truly see (Eph. 1:18); from which good or evil come (Luke 6:45)—the part that we must not lose (Prov. 4:23); the part that Christ came to heal, restore, and set free (Isa. 61). Your heart is the real you.

It is in your redeemed, made-new heart that your truest desires are stored. God said in the Old Testament, "I will give them an undivided heart and put a new spirit in them; I will remove from them their heart of stone and give them a heart of flesh. Then they will follow my decrees and be careful to keep my laws. They will be my people, and I will be their God" (Ezek. 11:19–20). In the New Testament this undivided heart and new spirit are described as coming from "God Who is all the while effectually at work in you [energizing and creating in you the power and desire], both to will and to work for His good pleasure and satisfaction and delight" (Phil. 2:13 AB). So we are instructed, "Whatever you do, work at it with all your heart" (Col. 3:23).

I can only touch on the idea of desire in this book. I highly encourage you to read John Eldredge's book *Desire* for much more concerning this topic.

Okay, desire is the key to understanding our glory or calling—not personality or spiritual gift indicators. And it will take understanding, discernment, shrewdness, and strength (in other words, maturity) in order to handle desire well. Because your glory is so significant to the Greater Story that we live in, much of what you have experienced in life has been an assault against your desires in order to shut them down or distance yourself from them. Most people I know would say that they really have no idea what they want, that they don't feel deeply about anything, and that the only thing they know they feel is lost, confused, and angry. So what do we do and what does God do with all of this?

AWAKEN, DEEPEN, FULFILL

> *Awake, awake, O Zion,*
> *clothe yourself with strength.*
> *Put on your garments of splendor [glory].(Isa. 52:1)*

God's call to His people has been, *Wake up and walk in your glory.* Wake up because most of us have deadened our desires. Not deadened as in they no longer exist, but rather as in the expression "he's dead to the world," as when someone is in a deep sleep, oblivious or unconscious to what's going on. You cannot kill your truest, deepest desires, for they are written into your very being—your heart—but you *can* sedate them. Therefore, there is a universal process that God takes us through with our desires in the development of our glory: He awakens desire, then He deepens desire, then He fulfills desire.[3] So much about our lives makes sense when we understand this process and so much clearer the journey becomes.

The inescapable, quintessential, overlooked truth is that God spends far more time awakening and deepening our desires than He spends fulfilling them. Why? Because God knows "the good man brings good things out of the good stored up in his heart" (Luke 6:45) and that "those with a noble and good heart, who hear the word, retain it, and [persevere]" (Luke 8:15) will bear fruit, "thirty, sixty or even a hundred times what was sown" (Mark 4:20). Far more time is spent planting and cultivating than harvesting. If we do not understand this, we will misinterpret a situation as failure when it doesn't result in some degree of fulfillment, when its purpose is to stir or cultivate our desires. As a child is tempted to discard his or her first seed project when it doesn't immediately sprout after being planted and watered, so we often exchange insight for disappointment.

AWAKENING

Years ago, I met a man who had recently been hired to start a ministry with people over the age of fifty. Because I had done some work on life stages, we spent some significant time together discussing what might be most helpful for this group. The conclusion we came to was that we needed to help this age group utilize all that they had experienced, learned, and acquired throughout their lives and walk with God by investing it generously in future generations. My heart was stirred for this kind of work during the same time that I was in a job with a completely different focus. Within days of the creation of this ministry strategy, this man asked me if I would consider leaving my current position to join him in this endeavor. So I went to my boss to inform him of our conversations and my intentions, to which he said, "Gary, that type of work is you, *but* that's not what this ministry is going to be about. It will focus on elder care, not calling." I knew he was sharing inside information that my friend didn't know yet. So I declined my friend's offer, feeling like this was some sort of cruel joke—being that close to something that I would love to do and having it disintegrate in my hands. In asking God what this whole thing was about, He responded with a question: "Did you feel that?" God will often give us a question rather than an answer because questions have the power to raise the motivations and issues of our hearts. Look at how many times Jesus responded to others with a question in Scripture. My immediate, unedited response was, "Yes! That's what I want to devote the rest of my life to." Then I sensed His response: "Wait and watch…. It's coming."

I remember being stirred by the little-known but profound movie *The Simple Life of Noah Dearborn*. It is the story of a man who lived out his glory, living unreservedly and generously in the brilliance and strength of his life. His purity, contentedness, and fruitfulness aroused in others either a desire to find their place in life or anger because they did not have what he had found. Though he was deeply intentional, humble, and kind with his life (a place that few people ever get to), there was more that he needed to learn about his heart. I watched this movie one evening and then again the next morning, and I have returned to it several times over the years. I came to understand that the story being told was more than just a good movie; God was up to something, and I knew it. He was awakening this deep, historic, long-standing desire in me to live and help others live a true, unambiguous, intentional life.

It is important that we stay alert to what God is awakening and that we don't undervalue or write it off as a waste of time. The awakening of desire is crucial to the journey we must take into our calling. But awakened desire is not sufficient to explain our lives. The apostle Paul said that in order for us to "[bear] fruit in every good work" (Col. 1:10), we must have "spiritual wisdom and understanding"

(v. 9). Often, our initial experience or understanding of our desires is not accurate. Desire is seldom what it first appears to be, so God must deepen our awakened desires.

DEEPENING

I explained in an earlier chapter how God revealed to me the desire *behind* my desire to run a gymnastics center. I thought my heart's desire was about a certain activity or job, which in my case was gymnastics. What God showed me was that what my heart desired was something *about* gymnastics, not the sport itself.

Jobs, positions, or locations are simply assignments into which we are to take the weightiness of our lives. God used gymnastics to awaken my heart's desires and my place with Athletes in Action to deepen them. But that was not the end of the deepening process; in fact, it was only the beginning. As my heart was released from my assignment with Athletes in Action, the deepening intensified. I had told my boss that I was leaving my position to find my new assignment. He graciously asked me to stay on for three more months to finish a project while I was looking for my next job. I expected that my "reassignment" would happen quickly since I was following God in this decision. But weeks and months passed with no offers, except one that I knew was not me. The job in question had nothing to do with what my life uniquely and powerfully had to offer and could be done only through my competency. So here was a test—would I hold steadfast to what God had shown me about who I was, or would I choose opportunity over leading, safety over risk?

Let me make two points of clarification here. First, I was able to provide for my family during that time. If that had not been the case and I had not heard from God otherwise, I would have taken a temporary job while on my expedition to our next place. Scripture says, "If anyone does not provide for his relatives, and especially for his immediate family, he has denied the faith and is worse than an unbeliever" (1 Tim. 5:8). Don't deny your faith by burdening your family financially in your attempt to follow your faith. Second, much of God's deepening work comes through tests and hardship. Scripture says that if we will face trials head-on, letting these trials accomplish their intended purpose, we will become "mature and complete, lacking in nothing" (James 1:2–4). In other words, all that you need to live the life you were meant for, you will have.

My intention, after leaving the interview and being told informally that I would be offered the job, was to keep that option available in case I didn't find anything else, in case God was a little too slow or got sidetracked. The next morning in my alone time with God I sensed Him say to me that if I did not let go of this job possibility, He would not lead me to my next assignment. So I called and withdrew my name. Within hours, I was called by a friend of a friend asking if I would be willing to interview for a job with the organization he worked for. In my heart I knew this was my next assignment, the next place in the Greater Story that God wanted for me regarding the glory of my life. I knew this assignment was right for me for two reasons: First, what the position was designed to accomplish, my life was designed to offer. And second, I heard God's "this is it," so I took the job.

Had I understood what the next year and a half of my life would be like, I might have chosen differently. Had I understood what the *result* would be, I would have been all the more enthusiastic and attentive. This is why Paul said, "*I pray that* the eyes of your heart may be enlightened, so that you will know what is the *hope* of His calling" (Eph. 1:18 NASB). We must stay in the hope and anticipation of what we will come to discover about our glory and about how our hearts will develop along the way.

In order to bring my desires to a place of greater clarity and purity, God caused me to live outside of them for a period of time. (The year and a half I was referring to.) Though I was hired to help associate organizations gain an understanding of their purpose, strategy, and stability in processes (a large part of my glory), I soon became lost in the labyrinth of public-policy issues. For the first year I was given books to read, tapes to listen to, staff to shadow, and meetings to observe, in order to learn what I needed to know about our stance on current public-policy issues. I was so isolated from the things I loved to do, and my heart was so drained by the pursuit of what I was unmoved by during this training period, I forgot who I was and what I most cared about.

During one of my training trips, I was sitting next to a prospective board member for one of our associate organizations. After our meal, the board chairman invited the board members to participate in a time of prayer to conclude our time together. The man I was talking to immediately jumped to his feet and started praying: "Dear God, help Gary endure this time of being unnoticed, underutilized, and disoriented; accomplish all that You have purposed for him through this." I had not told him what life had been like for me, but he described it perfectly as he prayed. God had sent me across the country to tell me that He was orchestrating all of this and that I needed to hang in there. And I did.

After a year and a half, what I knew of who I really was came back to me, and three profound things occurred. First, I realized that the contribution of my life and my calling was not dependent on the orchestration of another—as in being offered the perfect position. My calling was simply offering the weightiness of my life wherever I am. Second, I realized how deep and true, not simply circumstantial, were my desires to bring clarity, focus, and design to individuals and organizations. No matter how foggy and confusing circumstances became, I always returned to these core desires. Third, I became aware of when I was using my glory for selfish gain (recognition, inclusion, admiration, respect) versus when I was freely giving my life to another for his or her benefit. When you are able to detach and back up from your desires, you can observe them more honestly and see what has attached itself to them.

So, what we were created to do is written on our hearts in the form of our desires. This is why our hearts and desires have been and will continue to be assaulted. Because of the assault, God must continually awaken our desires. We must stay alert to what God is awakening, not undervaluing or writing it off as a waste of time. But awakening desire is not enough to instruct our lives. God must deepen our understanding of our desires. To live in the realm of desire, you must be cunning, not adolescent, for "the naive believes everything, but the sensible man considers his steps" (Prov. 14:15 NASB). Not every desire comes from a good and noble place. Nor is every desire as it first appears or is first experienced. God must bring our desires to a place of greater clarity and purity.

Chapter 8

INTERPRETING YOUR DESIRES

How we wish some sage, some person of extraordinary wisdom and insight who could fully understand our journey up to the current moment and possess more hope for our lives than we do, would say, "I will instruct you and teach you in the way you should go; I will counsel you and watch over you." To be understood at the deepest level by another whose heart is pure and safe, to have someone who will stick with you to the completion of your journey … this is what we want—this kind of direction and companionship.

So where can we find a person who can know us intimately and will guide us accurately? We do need such a person. It is God who has said, "I will instruct you and teach you in the way you should go; I will counsel you and watch over you" (Ps. 32:8). He knows what you were created to do. He knows what He has written on your heart in the form of your desires.

While working at a large Christian organization, I was approached by one of the executive vice presidents about leading a cabinet planning weekend. He said that he heard I was good at facilitating strategic planning. He told me that the president wanted all the cabinet members to be fully engaged in the planning and not distracted by the process. I asked him if I could give him an answer in the morning because I wanted time to pray about it, though something in me said I didn't need to pray about this, that it was an opportunity not to be missed. As I was driving home that evening, I asked Jesus if I should do this or not. He replied with a question: "If another organization asked you to do this for them, would you do it?" Instantly my heart replied, "No, I wouldn't really want to do that." Then a follow-up question arose: "Then why would you want to do this here?" Again, instantly an answer surfaced: "Because I would be in the inner circle, and they would see how much I have to offer." Until Jesus asked me these questions, I had no idea that this motivation for visibility and positional significance was at play in my heart.

God will guide us through deciphering the desires of our hearts. Jesus said, "Each tree is recognized by its own fruit.... The good man brings good things out of the good stored up in his heart" (Luke 6:44–45). The good we are to bring to the world is in our hearts, a treasure to be uncovered. Our glory can be recognized.

As Paul wrote to the believers in Thessalonica, "That is why we always pray for you, asking our God to help you live the kind of life he called you to live. We pray that with his power God will help you do the good things you want and perform the works that come from your faith" (2 Thess. 1:11 NCV). In the process of awakening and deepening the good things we want to do, where do we put our attention? What must we stay attuned to?

LISTENING TO YOUR HEART: DISCLOSURES OF DESIRE

Strength of Desire (Compelled Versus Concerned)

Throughout our lives we are exposed to many needs and issues that present themselves. Some of those needs we are able to quickly release, other issues may truly concern us, and a few may deeply move us. This is especially true of this era with the growing popularity of documentary/investigative-type shows and the Internet. We are blitzed daily by compelling information about homelessness, violence, evangelism, AIDS, education, addictions, political involvement, and poverty, to name just a few. All of these needs are noble, all are important, and all are timely. But the human heart can only carry so much need, and over time it has to release those things it was not created to pursue.

Then there are the needs or situations that we have never been able to fully dismiss. They haunt us. Everything seems to surface these needs and situations. We have "eyes and ears" for these things that others don't seem to have. We may find ourselves pulled to a particular topic area in bookstores. It's the subject of a news story where we turn the volume up and ask everyone to hush. It's the article we read two, three, maybe four times. I have been studying the subject of calling, not because calling has been work-related or I can't get any clarity on who I am, but rather out of deep desire and curiosity. Albert Einstein said, "Curiosity has its own reason for existing." There is a reason you are interested in certain things and not others. Your curiosity is linked to your truest desires.

Pay attention to your strength of desire. Your heart is revealing something important.

I remember going to a seminar on "retaining good employees." I was sent to this seminar because of my position as director of staff development. During the seminar the presenter showcased an approaching-middle-age waiter in a prestigious resort restaurant who had stayed in this position for seventeen years. While the audience accepted this example as a great employee retention technique, I was curious as to why this man had not moved on to something more true to who he was, something more challenging, more epic. As the seminar audience applauded the videotaped story, I became very upset, thinking, *Can't you see that this man is lost, stuck, resigned— you're not helping this man.* I couldn't let go of this man's story, and needless to say, the training seminar did not have its intended effect on me.

In fact, about six months later at work, I was warned that I was under scrutiny because several key employees who had left the organization stated in their exit interview that my teaching and conversations on calling had caused them to see that they needed to move on. This was seen as encouraging good employees to leave rather than creating a system to retain them for the company's sake. The vulnerable position I found myself in didn't matter to me; I was compelled to help people pursue and develop the glory of their lives and their assignment.

Scottish poet Robert Louis Stevenson said, "To know what you prefer, instead of humbly saying Amen to what the world tells you you ought to prefer, is to have kept your soul alive."[1] I have met many people who have lost their souls, their hearts, because they have been living a script someone else handed them. So many people have lived by the preferences of others because they have ignored their own hearts. Think about the man who goes into law practice because his father told him that's what he should do and then finds it hard to get up each morning to go to work and comes home angry each evening. Or what about the woman who works in a corporate office each day simply because she was told that this is what an intelligent, gifted woman should do to advance in life and be happy. But the truth is, for the past ten years she has been unhappy and has felt mostly loss as she has ignored her own desires.

What you were *created* to do is what you most *want* to do. Your calling in life comes in the form of your strongest desire, your truest preference, and is often initially experienced as your deepest curiosity. Your truest desire becomes compelling. The apostle Paul said, "I cannot boast, for I am compelled to preach. Woe to me if I do not preach the gospel!" (1 Cor. 9:16).

Let me clarify something at this point. I am not saying to let your life be led by emotions. But I am saying to be *aware* of your emotions, for they do speak of what may be going on in your heart or against your heart. You must, as with all things, live with both wisdom and revelation in order to correctly interpret your emotions. This is why you must look at both the strength of your desire and the consistency of desire as it presents itself in your life.

Consistency of Desire (Historic Versus Reactive)

What is true of you has always been true of you. What you were created to do has been in your DNA from the beginning. There is something unique that you have been able to see or understand or do throughout your entire life, regardless of its level of development.

My fascination and study of calling has stretched over twenty-five years. I have read most of the books on the subject that seemed credible to me. I have taken and analyzed most of the psychological instruments that are supposed to help people discover their calling. And, while in conversation with another person, this is where my mind always goes—their calling. For all but the recent year, I have not been paid to do this. I simply can't help it. It's been my heart's curiosity for half of my life.

C. S. Lewis said, "What I like about experience is that it is such an honest thing."[2] It is more honest than what is going on inside of you at any single moment. Every time I smell hot dogs being grilled I think, *I love hot dogs.* But experience informs me that I have never really liked them … especially a few moments after eating one or two. Your experience or personal history is a significant informant concerning your desires.

A man I met after one of our conferences told me of his frustration and disappointment with his career path. As he talked through his story, he told me of his love for music as a young boy. He had learned to play several instruments, but his most notable ability was to listen to a musical composition and be able to pick out each instrument's contribution to the piece. He could simply close his eyes, focus on each instrument, and understand how one musician was contributing to the others. His mother recognized and affirmed his unique ability, but his father diminished it as insignificant, having no relevance to life. This man pretty much walked away from music at that point, but his composer's heart was still there, though deep underground. Working through his story, he realized that in almost everything he had enjoyed doing, he was orchestrating a "piece of work" by picking up the contribution of each person and helping them understand their part in the final composition. The deepest, truest desire of this man's heart was to compose, orchestrate, and choreograph, and he discovered that these desires didn't necessarily have to be worked out in the realm of music. He realized that this was simply what he had been doing his entire life in any situation where he was free to do what he wanted to do. Orchestrating was his strongest and consistent desire. He emailed me months later with more clarity:

> *The idea of "transparent orchestration"—being used*
> *of God as his conduit in which I am transparent in*

the process—is what really makes my heart come
alive. This is true with leading worship and it was
also the case with the retreat I helped put together
last November with Dave.... I made it my mis-
sion to ensure that everything ran smoothly so that
Dave would be able to unleash his glory and that
there would be nothing hindering their ability to
meet with God in a powerful way. I could see how
much of my previous "smaller story" training as a
project manager was brought to bear: mitigating
risks, planning strategies, vendor negotiations, etc.
And during that whole time, I was amazed that I
never got stressed but rather felt like I was walking
with God, following His lead the entire time. It
was amazing.[3]

What you were created to do, the part you are to play, your truest desire will stand the test of time.

Stories of Desire (Books, Movies, Characters)

Your heart will also speak of the glory it possesses through the
stories you have loved and the characters that you have longed to be.

Leigh has always been moved by stories of emancipators. I
remember her reading stories to our children from the book *Great
Lives: Human Rights.* Even today, she continues to revisit those
biographies. One of her favorite stories in this book is about Chief
Joseph. He was the chief of the Nez Perce Indians, a very friendly and
noble people. These were the Indians who fed the starving Lewis and

Clark expedition and developed the famous Appaloosa pony, known for its great strength and courage in battle. Chief Joseph agreed with the United States government that he and his tribe would not harm settlers as long as they could be left undisturbed where they lived. But gold was found on their land, and greedy miners invaded their territory. The government decided that Chief Joseph must move his tribe to another state, which he refused to do for the sake of his people and a promise he made to his father.

The chief knew that the U.S. Army could destroy his tribe due to their numbers, so he decided to lead his people to Canada where they could be free. But the United States would not let them go. It was said that seldom in the history of warfare has there been leadership like that of Joseph. His forces numbered only two hundred warriors, many of them old and sick, and he also had six hundred women and children to take care of. Joseph's warriors had only a few rifles, along with their bows and arrows. The government troops had the finest modern weapons, including large cannons.

Not only did Chief Joseph's warriors fight skillfully and strategically, they fought nobly. They did not scalp the enemy; if they captured white women, they treated them gently and then released them; when they needed supplies, they paid for them; they did not destroy property; and they did not kill families of peaceful settlers along the way. Chief Joseph's heart and words inspired, bonded, and guided his people, especially in times of hardship. His voice stirred strength and perseverance in his people as he led them through the Rocky Mountains to Canada away from the pursuing U.S. troops. His Indian name, Heinmot Tooyalakekt, "Thunder Rolling in the

Mountains," accurately pictured the weightiness of his words and effect of his life.

Another story Leigh has loved and revisited throughout the years is the life of Corrie ten Boom—and her unshakable love for God and her tenacious struggle against the oppression and injustice brought against the Jews by Hitler. She was an emancipator, a liberator. If you have heard Leigh speak or had a conversation with her, you have probably felt her passion for people to be free and alive, especially when they have walked through great suffering. Through these stories, Leigh's heart is telling her something of her own role in this life, the part she has been created to play.

As I mentioned in the previous chapter, I was moved by the movie *The Simple Life of Noah Dearborn*. The movie begins with Noah making customized door trim for a historical building. While he was carving the trim out of a piece of solid oak, the foreman referred to him as a "carpenter god" because of his skill and precision. Something in me said, *That's what I want to be, that's what I want to help others become.* Not woodworkers or "carpenter gods," but people who know how to live in their splendor, to live in a way that the world sees as God-like. Noah was a man who knew what he was created to do; he understood the art that his life offered to the world; and he was unaffected by the expectations and seductions of others. Noah's life created in those around him the desire for the same clarity and *modus vivendi*—a manner of living, a way of life.

Another movie that I have loved is *The Legend of Bagger Vance*. I thought this movie was a story about golfers, but I was wrong. Instead, it's the story of a man (Rannulph Junah) who was coming into his glory and then lost it as he lost heart. But more importantly, the movie is about the awakening and deepening of a man's heart and desires through the pursuit and training by another (Bagger Vance). I'm not sure how many times I have watched this movie through the years, but each time something in me resonates with what Vance did for Junah—a part of me is validated and legitimized. Watching that movie heightens my desire for the same clarity Vance had and compels me to possess his *modus vivendi*.

Words of Desire

I have also noticed personally and with others that our hearts will resonate with certain words that express the effect our lives we're created to have.

Years ago while waiting for my son to finish his karate class, I went into a side room that had a dry-erase board on the wall. I drew a line down the center of the board and wrote all the things that I loved doing in the last five years on the left side. On the right side I wrote down the things that I did not enjoy doing no matter how well I did them. Then I looked for the core descriptive words in each column. I found the core words that described what I was doing when I was happy and most alive were the antithesis of the core words describing activities that brought me no life. Those core words from the left column were clarity, focus, design, and intentionality. I have lived with an awareness of these words for more than ten years, and they still resonate and excite my heart as I read them. These descriptive words are what I naturally want to bring to any situation I am in.

A year or so after doing this exercise, a friend suggested that I consider a position that recently had opened up. It was a CEO position for a nonprofit organization whose president had just published a popular book on calling. The position had all the environmental elements I would have wanted: It was an up-and-coming, fast-moving, and strategically thinking organization. It was a well-funded organization, had a nonreligious Christian founder and president, and had an emphasis on helping individuals and organizations seize their moment. The position required critical leadership responsibilities and had a generous compensation package as well. But as I put these words of desire against the reality of what I would be doing in this position, it became very apparent that the position was not for me, and I declined the interview process. Because I had words describing my truest desires in which to filter opportunities through, I was not as susceptible to the allure of position, visibility, association, and compensation.

LISTENING TO OTHERS—TOO CLOSE FOR CLARITY

Our glory is so personal to us, so "normal," that we barely see it. We don't see it as anything special or uncommon or extraordinary. Therefore we tend to overlook it, to dismiss it. We need others in our lives to spot our glory, to describe it, and to call it out.

I still to this day vividly remember what was said to me during the first days of my first full-time job after college. My boss said that I had the ability to see what was needed (clarity), to figure out how to best do it (design), and to get it done (focus and intentionality).

Years after that, a man whom I had been in conversation with said to me, "You have the ability to see a man's calling and the authority to call it out." Something in me said, "Really?" and then,

"Really!" You see, what I pick up in a person's story and what I see in his or her life is so enjoyable and relatively easy for me that I tend to undervalue and dismiss it.

This is why C. S. Lewis said, "In each of my friends there is something that only some other friend can fully bring out. By myself I am not large enough to call the whole man into activity."[4]

Not only is our glory hard to recognize because it is so natural to us, but it is also difficult because of the assault against it. Our friends can more fully see our glory because they are not under the same distancing, diminishing, disdaining, and disqualifying assault that we are under in regards to the glory of our lives. We have, as it were, night blindness where it is hard for us to see clearly with all the darkness that is coming against our lives. We need the eyes of others.

We really do need to "spur one another on toward love and good deeds" (Heb. 10:24) and "encourage each other every day … so none of you will become hardened because sin has tricked you" (Heb. 3:13 NCV).

LISTENING TO GOD
(WHAT ONLY GOD COULD TELL US)

Spirit of Wisdom and Revelation

The apostle Paul prayed that "God [will] fill you with the knowledge of his will through all spiritual wisdom and understanding … in order that you may live a life worthy of the Lord and may please him in every way: bearing fruit in every good work" (Col. 1:9–10).

God must give us a spirit of wisdom if we are to correctly interpret the things He has already written on our hearts and into our story. Anyone can discover these things, but without the "spirit of wisdom," there will be little to no understanding of how to handle them.

But wisdom is not enough; there are things you need to know that are still unknown, things that God must reveal. There are truths that only God would know about you—the realities of your situation and your future, things that He must speak to you. We can have pages of insights about our abilities, skills, goals, desires, and dreams and still be in the dark as to what to do next.

God is not running a job-placement agency or a personal-fulfillment task force in regards to our lives. His intention, as Dallas Willard said, is for us "to live as a co-worker with God in the creative enterprise of life on earth." God has set this whole story up, and He must and will speak personally to us regarding our part in it.

This is why Paul also prayed that God, "the Father of glory, may give to you a spirit of wisdom *and* of revelation in the knowledge of Him … that the eyes of your heart may be enlightened, so that you will know what is the hope of His calling" (Eph. 1:17–18 NASB).

The word *and* in this passage is really important. The mistaken extremes in the pursuit of one's calling are either relying exclusively on the "power" of wisdom or the "guarantee" of supernatural revelation.

The "wisdom" approach is what drives so many to the tests, indicators, and assessment tools. This usually comes from the stewardship approach to Christianity, the "do the best with what you have because one day you'll be held accountable" approach. But at its core, this approach comes from the belief that God does not or will not speak to us personally and intimately.

The revelation approach, at its extremes, believes that you wait for the next "word" from God about your life and simply walk in it—it's assured because God said it. As Graham Cook has so eloquently explained, prophetic words simply begin a process, a series of steps to guide you from where you are today to where God wants you to be. Often, prophecy declares the intention of God, not the inevitability of something.

Thomas à Kempis wrote,

> *You will never be devout of heart unless you are thus silent about the affairs of others and pay particular attention to yourself. If you attend wholly to God and yourself, you will be little disturbed by what you see about you.*
>
> *Where are your thoughts when they are not upon yourself? And after attending to various things, what have you gained if you have neglected self? If you wish to have true peace of mind and unity of purpose, you must cast all else aside and keep only yourself before your eyes.*[5]

So, "the good man brings good things out of the good stored up in his heart" (Luke 6:45). We can identify the "good things" (our glory, our effect) by looking for our strongest, most historic desires— the desires that compelled us and have stood the test of time. Your heart will also reveal its treasure through the stories you love, the characters you long to be, and the words you love to use.

However, our own observation is not complete or sufficient. We need the eyes of others who can see what we overlook as ordinary and who are not clouded by the spiritual warfare that we face. We really do need to "spur one another on toward love and good deeds" (Heb. 10:24).

And finally, God must give us a spirit of wisdom if we are to correctly interpret the things He has already written on our hearts and into our story. But wisdom alone is not enough—there are things that only God knows about us, our situation, and our future, things that He must reveal by His Spirit in order for us to understand our calling.

Chapter 9

STRENGTH TO HANDLE YOUR WEIGHTINESS

WE LIVE IN AN AGE OF GREAT EVENTS AND LITTLE MEN.
—Winston Churchill

The city of Los Angeles hosted the 1984 Summer Olympics. The world was watching what the entertainment capital of the world would do with the opening and closing ceremonies. During this time, I was running a gymnastics center in the L.A. area. The choreographers came to our gym asking if we had adult male gymnasts who could perform in the opening ceremonies. We had the gymnasts, and because of this,

I was given an incredible inside view of the entire production. The ceremonies were designed to be a truly epic event. Everything came off as planned except one thing … except one glorious moment designed and planned in the mind of the producer.

Toward the end of the opening ceremonies, an American bald eagle was to fly around the USC Coliseum over the heads of the audience while the national anthem was playing and then land on the Olympic rings at the end of the song.

The animal trainer for the event faced two significant problems while trying to make this moment happen. The first problem was locating an eagle in captivity. The second was only encountered after the first problem had been solved. The eagle the trainer found had been in captivity for six years because of injuries he had sustained. In order for this moment in the ceremony to be successful, a lot of restoration and training would need to take place before the big day.

After months and months of intense work, the time had come to test the eagle's training. He was brought to the Coliseum and released to fly. After several test flights the animal trainer encountered an unrecoverable problem.… The eagle died. An investigation found that the eagle had died as a result of vascular collapse and bacterial infection. Consequently, the untold millions who watched the show that summer day never experienced the beauty of that performance.

In a *TIME* magazine article written about the opening ceremonies, the animal trainer gave an epitaph to the eagle: "The eagle had been fat and coddled for years, and when finally called upon to behave like an eagle, he failed." Some deep part of me gasped. There was something transcendent about this story, something deeper and more profound than a glorious plan gone awry.

This is the story of many of our lives.

For all of us, there are divine moments we were created for. Moments created for our contribution, moments needing our glory. But often we are not prepared for what will be required of us. We have become fat and coddled, dull and untrained, Alert and Oriented Times Zero.

Erwin McManus wrote in *The Barbarian Way*,

> *We are not ready for the great challenges set before us. We have not been prepared to take on any great quest, to battle any great enemy, or even to pursue a great dream for which we have been born. Instead, Christianity has become our Shawshank, and our redemption will only come if we find the courage to escape the prison we have created for ourselves.*[1]

We were not meant to train for such challenges, quests, battles, or dreams alone. God has been with us, helping to develop us; and He is well aware of our injuries, our wounds, and our weaknesses. We have underestimated the power of our lives and our role in the story He has planned for us. But Satan has not underestimated us—that is why he launches such a fierce assault against our hearts. And neither does God—that is why He must train us.

DEEPER THAN ABILITY

When Scripture says that God is developing in us "the ability to do what pleases him" (Phil 2:13 ISV), I don't believe it is primarily talking about skill, understanding, or techniques. Those things can be easily acquired with all that is available to us—books, CDs, seminars and conferences, colleges and universities. You and I are fairly intelligent and competent people who can acquire most skills and understanding to a somewhat effective degree. If that's what was meant, we really wouldn't need God.

If ability could be defined in terms of spiritual gifts, which Scripture says every believer possesses, then why do so many believers live powerless or destructive lives? No, this is about something deeper, something more central to the glory within.

Possessing the "ability to do what pleases him" is about *becoming* the men and women who can handle the weightiness of their lives and the great mission they have been given.

The story we have been brought into is not a talent-show competition between Christians and non-Christians, which appears to be what many believe. We cheer and applaud when a musician, author, actor, singer, athlete, politician, or a movie producer steps forward to speak of his or her newfound faith in God. We unmercifully expect much and pray little for them, being naive to their probable inability to handle the weightiness of their decision, position, and life. There is an essential ability required, which is beyond talent.

SPECIAL OPS

As Winston Churchill faced an enemy, a regime, an advancing kingdom of darkness, he said, "We live in an age of great events and little men." His intent was not to belittle or disparage his countrymen, but rather to put into perspective the reality in which they lived and to call them up into it. For the times they were living in and the enemy they were facing, they needed to be more. They needed to become great men. Little men can have talent, but great men possess something more.

Jesus said, "I am sending you out like sheep among wolves. Therefore be as shrewd as snakes [wary, wise, cunning] and as innocent as doves [guileless, without falsity, pure]" (Matt. 10:16). As a shepherd, Jesus is not gathering us together and keeping the wolves at bay, He is actually sending us into the wolf packs. In order to accomplish our mission and survive, we must be cunning and without falsity.

We live behind enemy lines: "You do not belong to the world, … [God has] chosen you out of the world" (John 15:19). But Jesus prayed, "My prayer is not that you take them out of the world but that you protect them from the evil one…. As you sent me into the world, I have sent them into the world" (John 17:15, 18). Jesus was sent, commissioned, and deployed into this world with a great mission, a great purpose. He has sent each of us into this world in the same way.

We are called to be Special Operations forces, which are "specially organized, trained forces to achieve military, political, economic, or informational objectives by unconventional means in hostile, denied, or politically sensitive areas."[2]

This talk of mission, an enemy, war, training, and preparation is not bravado, hype, or an attempt to inspire. The mission is real, as is the glory of your life.

A TRAINED HEART

So what does a trained heart look like? What is true of a person who can handle well the weightiness of his or her life? What is this "ability" that goes deeper than talent?

Dallas Willard said, "God's purpose is to bring us to the point, through the development of our character, where He can empower us to do what we want to do." God implants and develops deep desires in our hearts that compel us to do what we were created to do. At the same time, He deepens and expands our capacity to carry those desires in a powerful and effective way. God wants to enable us to walk in our glory, but only as we have the ability to possess and to offer it.

When my kids were young, they wanted to drive my car. I understood their desire, but I could not let them drive until they had developed the *capacity* to drive. They would not be able to drive until they could reach the accelerator and the brake and see over the steering wheel … until reaction time was developed … and until they had focus, perspective, and a driver's permit. When these things were developed, I could then empower them to do what they wanted to do by lending them my car.

The apostle Paul yearned for people to get to this place spiritually when he wrote, "I urge you to live a life worthy of the calling you have received. Be completely humble and gentle; be patient, bearing with one another in love" (Eph. 4:1–2).

There is an enormous amount of power in true humility, gentleness, patience, and love! So many times I offered the weightiness of my life without these qualities, and as needed as my offering may have been, it was instead unhelpful and somewhat destructive.

When our family moved to Colorado from Southern California, two men entered my life. One of these men was Paul Stanley, a man who poured into me week after week, year after year. Paul's passion and brilliance centered on personal development and leadership. The other man, Brent Curtis, poured into my life his zeal and insight concerning the heart through our times together in our covenant group, counseling times, and vacations. The glory of their lives has played a significant role in developing mine. These men revealed many things to me that God had revealed to them, things I needed and have in turn offered to others. But perhaps their greatest contribution to my life was the manner in which they brought their revelation and strength from God to my life—through humility, gentleness, patience, and love.

But like anything that is true, powerful, and life giving, these things are acquired over time, are hard won, and may have counterfeits.

HUMILITY

I read once that the word *humility* was coined by Christians. The Romans and Greeks did not have a word for humility; they despised the attitude that it held. Humility is similar to the word *glory* in that it is frequently used in Scripture, is absolutely essential in our walk with God and with others, and is highly misunderstood.

Scripture says, "Do nothing out of selfish ambition or vain conceit, but in humility consider others better than yourselves. Each of you should look not only to your own interests, but also to the interests of others" (Phil. 2:3–4).

"Do nothing out of selfish ambition." Ambition, the desire to be excellent at something, is not the issue. The danger is "selfish ambition," which is the desire to be better than others so that you will have more than them—more visibility, notoriety, appreciation, recognition, authority, or financial rewards. *Selfish ambition* literally means to contend with another, to put oneself forward.

Not only does Paul attach the word "selfish" to "ambition," but he couples it with the phrase "vain conceit," which is translated by the King James Version as "vainglory." The desire to live out your glory is good. In fact, as mentioned in an earlier chapter, Paul says in Romans 2:7, "[God] will give eternal life to those who keep on doing good, seeking after the glory and honor and immortality that God offers" (NLT). The danger is "vainglory," which is literally groundless or empty splendor.

Selfish ambition and vainglory both want to be seen as brilliant, invaluable, gifted, powerful, and major players. These traits are about seeing ourselves or our interests as primary in the world. Selfish ambition and vainglory are about what others will give me because of my glory, instead of what others will receive because of my glory. It is, in Larry Crabb's words, "spiritual prostitution"—using our giftedness to get what we want, using it for something other than what is was intended for.

It is commonly believed that humility is seeing oneself as unimportant or unnecessary, having little or nothing to offer, and perhaps being more of a liability than an asset to the kingdom of God. On the contrary, humility is seeing that you have been given something extraordinary that others will need. Paul poses the question, "What do you have that was not given to you? And if it was given to you, why do you brag as if you did not receive it as a gift?" (1 Cor. 4:7 NCV). You have been given something glorious that the world needs, so don't diminish and disregard it. Receive and offer it as a gift from God to you and for others.

Maybe some of you are thinking, *What about the verse, "Do not think of yourself more highly than you ought, but rather think of yourself with sober judgment" (Rom. 12:3)?* The antidote for conceit or arrogance is not self-deprecation; it is instead sober judgment. Sobriety is a fascinating phrase and metaphor to use. When a person is intoxicated (under the influence of alcohol) he tends to either overestimate his abilities, intelligence, appearance, and impact—or underestimate them. Someone who is intoxicated often becomes more exaggerated or withdrawn, and either way, he is not thinking of himself as he ought.

Our judgment can be impaired by being under the influence of many things other than alcohol or drugs—like fear, pride, shame, hurt, accusation, or confusion. As we live under these influences, we will tend toward exaggeration or diminishment.

I can remember so vividly (because it has happened so frequently) sitting silent in meetings for hours ... not because I was taking it all in or had nothing of significance to offer to the meeting, but because I was under the influence of fear. I thought that no one really wanted me there or wanted what I had to offer. It wasn't until a friend said to me, "I don't know where you went, but we need you here offering what you see and know—you are needed." His admonition was like a strong cup of coffee or a cold shower jolting me out of a drunken stupor.

Humility is about owning who you are, your glory—your splendor, strength, weightiness, beauty, abundance. Humility does not exaggerate, nor does humility make oneself smaller.

Phillips Brooks said, "The true way to be humble is not to stoop until you are smaller than yourself, but to stand at your real height against some higher nature that will show you what the real smallness of your greatest greatness is."[3]

It was reported that before retiring to bed, Theodore Roosevelt would often gaze at the sky, searching for a tiny patch of light near the constellation of Pegasus and recount, "It is as large as our Milky Way. It is one of a hundred million galaxies. It consists of one hundred billion suns, each larger than our sun." Then he would walk to his bedroom saying, "Now I think we are small enough."[4]

In this world and story that we live in, there are always counterfeits to everything that is good and true. A counterfeit is something made as an imitation so as to be passed off fraudulently or deceptively as genuine.

The counterfeit of humility is shame, which is often misunderstood and accepted as humility. Shame is the painful feeling, valid or invalid, of unworthiness, disgrace, or contempt. These feelings of shame can create very similar appearing behaviors externally as humility does. But the effect of shame is the belief that "I am nothing and have nothing to offer," causing a person to rarely exert him or herself or take risks, and always offer disclaimers or apologies when sharing with others. So, many people stay in a place of shame, despite the powerful, all-inclusive work of Christ, and falsely believe this is what it means to walk in humility.

HUMILITY IS A CORE STRENGTH

As I said earlier, the Romans and the Greeks despised the concept of humility. They saw it as embracing and elevating weakness, inadequacy, and vulnerability. And while this is true of humility, it is more truly an unequivocal strength. We see our weaknesses, inadequacies, and vulnerabilities that cause us to rely on God for our lives, and relate to others with compassion. Humility also makes us alert, cunning, shrewd, steady, astute, and wise—essential attributes and skills for living behind enemy lines.

"A man's pride will bring him low, but a humble spirit will obtain honor" (Prov. 29:23 NASB), Scripture says, and "Let him who thinks he stands take heed that he does not fall" (1 Cor. 10:12 NASB).

As we discover and develop our glory, we become vulnerable to two dangers: false reliance and harshness. There is so much joy experienced in living in and giving out our glory, that we can unconsciously shift our reliance off of God and on to our calling in life. We start to believe that walking in our calling is walking with God, but this is not necessarily true. Many times in the busyness of offering my strength, I have found myself wondering when I last spent set-apart time with God. Much like when I drive my car, getting things done, only to later wonder, "How long have I been driving on empty?" Or what about enjoying the blessing and security of a good marriage and then wondering how long it has been since we went out on a date together? When we begin to walk in a place of this kind of self-reliance, we are very vulnerable to the Enemy and the trap of operating out of our own strength. We must realize that we are never enough.

When our strength, beauty, and the abundance of our lives are discovered and developed, we can also become harsh with others in the areas where we have succeeded. We find it so easy or natural to operate in our glory (i.e., organizing, encouraging, discerning, clarifying, nurturing, comprehending, connecting) that we become critical and unsympathetic toward those who struggle. So we either do not offer our strength to those who "aren't trying hard enough," or we offer our strength with contempt and frequently do more damage than good.

HUMILITY IS THE CORE OF WISDOM

WHEN PRIDE COMES, THEN COMES DISGRACE,
BUT WITH HUMILITY COMES WISDOM.
—Proverbs 11:2

Thomas à Kempis wrote, "They who are still new and inexperienced in the way of the Lord may easily be deceived and overthrown unless they guide themselves by the advice of discreet persons.... Seldom do they who are wise in their own conceits bear humbly the guidance of others."[5]

So much wisdom is required for us to live well in this life and in our particular role; learning is a never-ending process. Most of what we learn will come from others. Experience, by itself, is not sufficient. A piece of wisdom a friend shared with me was, "We do not learn from experience; we learn from evaluated experience." It's so true. Many people have years of accumulated experience but little wisdom. As Proverbs 13:10 says, "Wisdom is with those who receive counsel" (NASB).

It is the truly humble (not those living in shame) who can ask profoundly important questions (going from vulnerable to deeply vulnerable) like:

> Was I helpful?

> How did I do? How did it go?

> Why do you think it didn't go as well as it could have? Why do you think it went well?

> How would you describe me?

> What am I like when I'm "not myself"?

> What was my effect on you (or the group)?

> What do you think I'm unaware of? What do I need to know or understand?

> What I am like to be around (as a friend, spouse, coworker, boss)?

Years ago my mentor and I, along with several other men, created a program called Halftime Journey based off the book *Halftime* by Bob Buford. Through a year of meetings across the United States, we put together a seven-month mentoring curriculum and an introductory seminar. At the first seminar I watched the audience hang on every word Paul (my mentor) spoke. Their eyes had that look of fascination, clarification, and admiration. When I spoke, their reaction was not quite the same. It felt more like, "Who is this guy, what does he have to tell me, and when does Paul come back up?" After that first evening when we were back at the hotel room, I apologized to Paul for blowing it and asked him what I did wrong. He told me that the only difference between us when we spoke was that he spoke as a fifty-year-old and I spoke as a forty-year-old. Then he gave me a very sage piece of advice: "Just be who you are, it is good and it is enough; when you are fifty, you will have the effect of a fifty-year-old when you speak." Through Paul's words I realized how much I was striving to act older than I was and saw the self-created expectations and pressures I was living under. Paul gave me much-needed permission to simply be myself. As Ralph Waldo Emerson wrote, "Envy is ignorance. Imitation is suicide."

A person with true humility is open and searches for the wisdom and guidance of others. This is how we become "shrewd [cunning] as snakes and as innocent [unmixed] as doves."

HUMILITY IS THE PATH TO BECOMING UNMIXED

As C. S. Lewis pointed out, "the more we get what we now call 'ourselves' out of the way and let Him take us over, the more truly ourselves we become.... The more I resist Him and try to live on my own, the more I become dominated by my own heredity and upbringing and surroundings and natural desires. In fact what I so proudly call 'Myself' becomes merely the meeting place for trains of events which I never started and which I cannot stop."[6]

Only through humility can we look honestly at our behavior, our inner life, and begin to understand all of the things that are motivating us. Unexamined and unaddressed, we truly become dominated by many of the painful things that happened to us, even decades ago. We see this force in our lives when we overreact to something we see or something said to us, or just to a person's presence. We wonder, "Why do I do that every time I am in this situation—I don't want to." We become something or someone we are not. We are "mixed."

For years I wondered why, when I got into some sort of a social gathering, I would start to become uncomfortable, awkward, and withdrawn, even with good friends. I hated what I became in those gatherings. No matter how hard I tried, I couldn't stop that "train," as C. S. Lewis described it. After conversations with others, with my heart, and with God, I discovered a prevailing message that had been painfully delivered deep into my heart as a child: "If you don't have something to offer, then I don't want to be with you." In a social situation (versus a work situation), nothing was required or needed from me other than my presence and heart, and that induced and amplified the thought that people really didn't want to be with me. It wasn't until I realized what was going on in my heart, what was at play, that I could resist the lie with the truth that the greatest thing I had to offer was my heart, and my heart was valuable and enjoyable to others.

I often find myself sliding from being discerning and perceptive to being cynical and sarcastic ... from picking up what is going on under the surface, to distrusting another's motives. I hate it when I become that person; it's not the truest thing about me. It wasn't until several people brought this tendency toward cynicism and sarcasm to me (the eyes of others) that I took a hard, in-depth look at myself. And then God, in His creativity, brought me in front of several very cynical and sarcastic people and asked me, "How do you like it?" I didn't; it was awful. Usually these tendencies are not something you can simply stop by an act of your will, so I dug deeply into my heart and story to find the root of my reactions in certain situations.

One point of origin that I discovered was from a moment in my childhood that I wrote about earlier in this book. It was when a neighbor boy broke my Rifleman Rifle I had gotten for Christmas. At that moment, a mistrust or suspicion of people's motives took root in my heart. This root of mistrust would later start to define my behavior in ways that I did not want. As God showed this to me, I asked Him to heal this wounded part of me. I confessed and renounced my agreement that people would always be willing to destroy what I care about, and as a result, I became less cynical and more discerning in my life.

Without humility, there is no gentleness. In humility, we realize that every person is in a battle for his or her life.

GENTLENESS

As I mentioned earlier, we can develop a harshness, an impatience, a type of heartlessness with others in the areas where we have strength, abundance, and splendor. We speak or act with passion with what we are offering, but not with compassion to the hearts of those whom we are giving. We forget that God has given us in abundance, and we are to then give help to those who have not. We forget that where we are today and what we have to offer was developed and honed over time and through trial and error.

Without gentleness, little of what we genuinely have to offer will be received. How is gentleness developed? Gentleness is usually developed through hardship, struggle, failure, disappointment, and sorrow.

Oswald Chambers said, "Sorrow burns up a great amount of shallowness…. You always know the man who has been through the fires of sorrow…. If a man has not been through the fires of sorrow, he is apt to be contemptuous."[7]

This is so true. The man or woman who has not gone though much hardship and sorrow and who has not embraced the reality of it tends to be impatient with the weaknesses or difficulties of others. The person who has gone through the fires of sorrow has burned off the shallow belief that life is simple and just a matter of making right choices.

Paul asked the Romans, "Do you show contempt for the riches of his kindness, tolerance and patience, not realizing that God's kindness leads you toward repentance?" (2:4). Instruction, help, correction, and rescue are much easier to receive when they are given with gentleness.

However, there is a counterfeit to gentleness, and it is *fear*. The fear to offer yourself—what you can do, what you see, hear, know. It's the fear that you might "do it wrong" or that you will be ignored, rejected, ridiculed. In fear you do and say nothing, and this can be misread as gentleness, when in fact it is the simple absence of your weighty presence.

One of the ways I have found that the Enemy instigates this counterfeit in my life is by presenting two options when I see a situation in which my understanding could be needed. The first option is to say it forcefully, out of anger, belligerently, antagonistically—out of the belief that they don't want to hear from me in the first place. Knowing that this will not be effective and that this is not the kind of man I want to be, I am then presented with the second option: to do or say nothing. Given those two options, saying nothing seems like the right way to go. Of course it is evident that both of these options are fear based. There is an alternative—speaking gently without antagonism while giving the appropriate weightiness to my words and using the passion required by the moment: "For God has not given us a spirit of fear and timidity, but of power, love, and self-discipline" (2 Tim. 1:7 NLT).

This brings us to the third vital skill required: patience. Without humility and gentleness, there is no patience.

PATIENCE

> PATIENCE: THE ABILITY TO ENDURE WAITING,
> DELAY, OR PROVOCATION ... OR TO PERSEVERE
> CALMLY WHEN FACED WITH DIFFICULTIES.
> —*Encarta World English Dictionary*

We must have patience with the mystery of life. As quoted earlier, Søren Kierkegaard said, "Life can only be understood backward; but it must be lived forward." We must have patience with God's work in our lives; as Oswald Chambers said, "The test is to believe that God knows what He is after."[8]

We must have patience in our offering to others; as Scripture says, "Clothe yourselves with humility toward one another, because, 'God opposes the proud but gives grace to the humble.' Humble yourselves, therefore, under God's mighty hand, that he may lift you up in due time. Cast all your anxiety on him because he cares for you" (1 Peter 5:5–7).

To be as shrewd as snakes and as innocent as doves, we must not be rash or hasty, impulsive or compulsive. In humility we can wait and watch for God's timing, His movement, and His intervention. In humility, we allow our hearts and the hearts of others to respond as they are able—as opposed to arranging, manipulating, demanding, and controlling the response of another.

When God brought me to a place and position of hiddenness and lostness in my journey, I quickly became impatient and determined to walk into my destiny—now—not believing that God knew what He was after. I attended an in-house workshop on leadership development offered by the organization I was working with. At the conclusion of the class, the speaker said that if anyone was interested in helping teach these workshops to let her know. It appeared that this was my break, the proverbial "open window" that I was to walk through. So that evening, as I was walking from the bathroom sink to the bed, I told God that tomorrow morning I was going to walk into the staff development director's office and tell her that I was the man for the job, that this was why God brought me here.

As soon as I finished my thought/prayer/statement of intent, God spoke very clearly to me. He said, "If you exalt yourself, I will humble you; if you humble yourself, I will exalt you in due time" (Matt. 23:12, author's paraphrase). I had no doubt this was God speaking to my heart because I lack success in memorizing Scripture, and I had not been looking for a reply like that. In fact, I was not looking for any response from God. I was so startled by God's admonition that I chose not to debate with Him. In those moments my heart blurted out, "I don't want to be humiliated any further." So I dropped the idea altogether and never thought of it again. This story concluded seven years later when I was asked by the vice president of HR to take the position of director of staff development. It wasn't until several years later that I realized God had exalted me at the proper time.

Though I wanted to seize the moment and "make it happen" right away after the workshop, I was nowhere near the man that I would be seven years later. I had to be patient—to endure waiting, to persevere calmly when faced with difficulties. I had to wait for the proper time, even though I had no idea when that was, and believe that God knew what He was after.

There is a time for everything; therefore we must patiently wait so that we may understand what this time is all about for us and for others.

> *There's an opportune time to do things, a right*
> *time for everything on the earth:*
> *A right time for birth and another for death,*
> *A right time to plant and another to reap,*
> *A right time to kill and another to heal,*
> *A right time to destroy and another to construct,*

A right time to cry and another to laugh,

A right time to lament and another to cheer,

A right time to make love and another to abstain,

A right time to embrace and another to part,

A right time to search and another to count your losses,

A right time to hold on and another to let go,

A right time to rip out and another to mend,

A right time to shut up and another to speak up,

A right time to love and another to hate,

A right time to wage war and another to make peace. (Eccl. 3:1–8 MSG)

We may clearly and accurately see the need, but we must first understand the moment: "The wise heart will know the proper time and procedure" (Eccl. 8:5).

The counterfeit to patience is resignation or disengagement. A person can appear to be so patient with themselves or others when, in reality, they have just given up on the hope of change. It is only the patient man or woman who is comfortable with mystery and can actually enjoy the process of God's orchestration. As C. S. Lewis said, "The tuning up of the orchestra can be itself delightful, but only to those who can in some measure, however little, anticipate the symphony."[9]

SOFT SKILLS?

When I worked in the HR field, these qualities (humility, gentleness, patience) were referred to as "soft skills." I really disliked this term because to me it implied that they were nice but not necessary, like accessories—not the real deal, just add-ons. When budget constraints dictated that we drop unnecessary efforts, "soft-skill training" was targeted first.

In many ways humility, gentleness, and patience are hard skills. They are "hard" versus "soft" in that they are absolutely critical to our survival and success. They are characteristic of the life that is worthy of its calling (Eph. 4:1–2), and they are the fruit of the Spirit (Gal. 5:22–23).

Humility, gentleness, and patience are "hard" skills in that they are difficult to acquire. Goethe, the German poet wrote, "Talent develops in quiet places, character in the full current of human life." It is in our day-to-day living that humiliation calls forth humility; that the fires of sorrow burn up shallowness; and that waiting, delay, and provocation cultivate patience.

As God was delivering His people out of bondage and guiding them into the land and life that He had created for them, He said that they would not completely possess the land "until [they had] increased enough to take possession of the land" (Ex. 23:30). It is the same for us—God must increase us (our character) to the point where we can fully possess the glory that He has given us.

So we typically underestimate the power of our lives and our role in the Greater Story. Satan does not—and that is why he launches such a fierce assault against our hearts and desires. And neither does God—that is why He must train us. We live behind enemy lines. As Jesus was commissioned and deployed into this world with a great mission by His Father, so have we been thus commissioned.

God implants and develops deep desires in our hearts that compel us to do what we were created to do. At the same time, He deepens and expands our capacity to carry those desires in a powerful and effective way. God wants to enable us to walk in our glory, but only as we have the ability (a trained heart) to possess and to offer it. We have that ability when our hearts are in a place of humility, gentleness, and patience (Eph. 4:1–2).

Humility is fully owning and offering your true glory—your splendor, strength, beauty, weightiness, and abundance. Humility does not exaggerate or deny what one possesses. It is through humility that we are open to the wisdom and guidance of others. It is through humility that we look honestly at our lives, behavior, and motivations—and how we become "shrewd [cunning] as snakes and as innocent [unmixed] as doves."

Without gentleness, little of what we authentically have to offer will be received. Gentleness is usually developed through hardship, struggle, failure, disappointment, and sorrow. We must remember that what we have been given in abundance (our glory) is for the sake of others, and the person we are today has been developed and honed over time and through trial and error.

To operate behind enemy lines, we must also have patience. We must be able to wait and watch for God's timing, His movement, and His intervention—allowing our hearts and the hearts of others to respond as they are able, as opposed to arranging, manipulating, demanding, and controlling the response of another. We must have patience with the mystery of life. We may clearly and accurately see an opportunity, but we must first understand the moment—"The wise heart will know the proper time and procedure" (Eccl. 8:5).

Chapter 10

BETWEEN DESIRE
AND FULFILLMENT

IT TAKES A LONG TIME TO BRING
EXCELLENCE TO MATURITY.
—Publilius Syrus

It is often our hope and also a clear misunderstanding that a few
fortunate people get to be an exception to the challenging process
of "becoming." Our mistake is believing that some find their calling quickly and easily. Our hope is that perhaps we get to be the
exception to the long, arduous process of discovering our glory

and developing into the person whom God can empower to do what he or she wants to do. We hope for an epiphany with a miraculous transformation.

When you look at the truly great men and women whose lives are chronicled in Scripture, you can see the process or journey they had to take to become who they were created to become. Take David, for instance. It is said of David, "[God] brought him from tending the sheep so he could lead the flock, the people of Jacob, his own people, the people of Israel. And David led them with an innocent heart [with integrity of heart] and guided them with skillful hands" (Ps. 78:71–72 NCV). In other words, God used the years of shepherding sheep with all of its particular skills and hardships to impart to David a trained heart and trained hands so that he could do what God had created him to do. David was not an exception to the journey.

If anyone might have been the exception, it would have been Jesus. But it was said of Jesus that He "grew in wisdom and stature [physical maturity], and in favor with God and man" (Luke 2:52). So He was not an exception to the process either. Jesus said, "A student is not above his teacher, but everyone who is fully trained will be like his teacher" (Luke 6:40). We must be fully trained, becoming more like Jesus, and take the place in the Greater Story that we have been created for.

There is no special anointing or prophetic promise that will get us around the discovery and development process. In fact, all prophecy simply begins a process—a journey taking us from where we are to where God wants us to be. There are no shortcuts, but we can create delays and detours.

THE BEAUTY OF "SPONTANEOUS" BRILLIANCE

I absolutely love the moments in life when people are spontaneously brilliant. I am left spellbound when talented musicians or singers start ad-libbing, playing off each other, making it up as they go. I am fascinated when gifted counselors can lead a person through an informal, impromptu conversation right to the core issue in his or her life. I'm enthralled when a person is asked an unscripted question and answers with transcendent, almost poetic insight, offering more than was expected but what was profoundly needed. All of these people may say, "It was just God," but I would bet it has been "just God" training them over years until "Christ is formed in [them]" (Gal. 4:19). A person's brilliance in the moment is the fruit of hours upon hours of experience and discipline.

According to Dan Sullivan, "Studies of great performers in all fields support a general rule that it takes about 10,000 hours of repetition, experimentation and innovation before a unique ability will translate itself into a genius-like activity."[1]

Not only will the discovery and development of our glory—the strength, beauty, abundance, brilliance, weightiness of our lives—take time, experience, and discipline, it will also take perseverance. Perseverance is "the characteristic of a man who is not swerved from his deliberate purpose and his loyalty to faith and piety by even the greatest trials and sufferings."[2] Our calling, our real life … is hard-won.

The apostle Paul said, "I press on to take hold of that for which Christ Jesus took hold of me" (Phil. 3:12). In other words, we are to strenuously pursue God's purpose for our lives until it is fully realized. It will not be quick or easy, but it will be gloriously and joyously worth it.

THE REST OF THE STORY

Throughout this book, I have given you glimpses of my journey since boyhood. But now let me bring you into the last several years of my pilgrimage.

The year before I left Focus on the Family as the director of staff development, I was walking around the grounds praying on a beautiful summer day. Though I loved the work I was doing and the people I worked with, I had a growing sense that God was about to bring me into something new. As I was praying, I sensed God say that He was going to join John Eldredge's calling with mine into a ministry that would be the fruit of Brent Curtis's life. Brent was the coauthor of *Sacred Romance* with John Eldredge, and the three of us and our wives had met together for years. Brent died tragically in a rock-climbing accident during one of our first men's retreats.

I never said a word about this conversation with God to anyone. Many months later, John and Stasi asked Leigh and me to join them in the development of what is now known as Ransomed Heart Ministry. It was one of the most exciting, challenging, intimate, and fulfilling places I had ever worked. The early years required everything of me that I wanted to offer as we developed the direction, organization, message, and methodology for the ministry. I was using my love for "clarity, focus, and design" both with the organization and individuals. It was a place where I continued to develop this message on "calling" and where Leigh and Stasi developed the first women's retreat, then known as Ransomed Femininity, which later became Captivating. I remember telling the younger staff one afternoon that they would have many more assignments and missions in their lifetime, but that this was probably my final one because it fit so well.

Though I had been studying and speaking on calling for twenty years, the material was formalizing into two successive retreats and possibly into a book. By my fifth year with Ransomed Heart, I was doing six to ten calling retreats a year on my personal time outside of the ministry. By year seven, this had become too big and I had become too passionate, too compelled to do this "on the side" anymore. Several of the staff who attended a calling retreat suggested in a meeting that this become one of the "advanced" retreats that Ransomed Heart offers. I said nothing, nor did the others. The silence conveyed an uncomfortably clear answer. A month or so later, during a prayer and fasting time at Ransomed Heart, I asked God if there was something He wanted to say to me. "Read the beginning of Ecclesiastes, chapter three." I opened my Bible and then God said, "I will tell you what season you are entering into." It reads like this:

> *There is a time for everything, and a season for*
> *   every activity under heaven:*
> *a time to be born and a time to die,*
> *   a time to plant and a time to uproot,*
> *a time to kill and a time to heal,*
> *   a time to tear down and a time to build,*
> *a time to weep and a time to laugh,*
> *   a time to mourn and a time to dance,*
> *a time to scatter stones and a time to gather them,*
> *   a time to embrace and a time to refrain,*

> *a time to search and a time to give up,*
>   *a time to keep and a time to throw away,*
> *a time to tear and a time to mend,*
>   *a time to be silent and a time to speak,*
> *a time to love and a time to hate,*
>   *a time for war and a time for peace. (Eccl. 3:1–8)*

As I was reading this scripture, God told me that I was coming into a time when something was going to die so that something could be born, a time of uprooting so that something could be planted, a time of tearing down, scattering, mourning and giving up. These words were not comforting, but God's forewarning was because I believed that if He was telling me what was coming, then He would be with me in it. I kept these words to myself so as not to create or manipulate circumstances. And during the next six months this scripture was fulfilled.

Several months after receiving this scriptural forecast from God, I explained to the other men on the leadership team, my closest friends, that God had brought me to the point where I must develop and speak this message full-time—that this is what I must do, for this is who I am. Though they supported what I was doing with this message of calling, their response was clear: John's writing was to be front and center to Ransomed Heart; therefore this was not an option. So to stay true to what God had shown me about who I was and what I was to do, I had to leave.

Oswald Chambers wrote, "If the Spirit of God has stirred you, make as many things inevitable as possible, let the consequences be what they will."[3] I had to make God's stirring to speak, counsel, train, and write on calling as inevitable as possible. The only way I could do that was to start a new ministry—The Noble Heart. It was now time for the other side of the Ecclesiastes equation—planting, birthing, building, gathering, searching, and healing.

By the time this book is published, it will have been two years since I started The Noble Heart. These years have been the most thrilling and fulfilling as well as the most disconcerting and vulnerable.

There is nothing like creating a situation where you can fully pursue your desires and dreams to cause you to second-guess how accurate your perception and understanding has been. Reality is far more disrupting than dreaming.

At this initial point, I was working by myself out of my home, wondering how all this was going to happen. One morning during my time with God, I asked Him what my vulnerabilities were. The answer rose in my heart: overworking to prove yourself right in your decision and working alone so as to never suffer this pain again. I knew this was God's answer because it was absolutely true and not what I wanted to hear. But, as I said before, clarity is not restoration, so with this warning, I continued to work ten to twelve hours a day fairly isolated. I loved what I was developing and doing, but my heart was growing weary.

Then, one day while I was in a phone meeting, I glanced over at my bookshelf. On one shelf were two prints that I have loved for years. One is a painting of four men riding across a river on a crisp, golden fall morning dressed in dusters and cowboy hats. The other is a picture of a lone Indian on his horse with his headdress and bow leaning forward in his saddle on a frosty gold-lit fall morning. As my ear was on the phone and my eyes on the pictures, God asked me which life I wanted—to work alone or with others. I needed to choose. At that moment, I chose to walk and work with others. So, through time on the phone and the creation of "tribal gatherings," I had a new fellowship, a new posse. I heard Graham Cook say that sometimes God will call you somewhere where your friends cannot go, and there He will provide new friends. This is so true—it's part of the journey. We cannot become what we need to be by remaining where and what we are. There is "a time to embrace and a time to refrain."

It was also within the first year that an acquaintance emailed me about meeting over lunch to discuss the publishing of my material on calling. I had been burned by one book agent and singed by another, so my publishing aspirations had been reduced to a photocopied, spiral-bound manuscript for those who requested one. This acquaintance, now a good friend, works for David C. Cook Publishing. He asked if he could present a book proposal on my material to his publishing board, which he did at what turned out to be the beginning of the recent recession. I was prepared to return to my copy-center manuscript vision when I got an email from him: *How about we publish your book?*

What is important to know about this story is that my close friend, Bart Hanson, said that he believed my separation from Ransomed Heart would bring about the fulfillment of this book, and it did. You see, there is a time for things to die and a time to be birthed.

"LIVE LIKE AN ARTIST"

Shortly after that, I awoke in the middle of the night worried by the uncertainties in my life—*Am I doing what I'm supposed to do? Am I where I'm supposed to be? Am I doing life the right way? Are my motives right?* I decided to go into another room so I could pray out loud and journal my thoughts with God. After forty minutes of mumbling and stumbling my way into the issues of my heart, God answered me with one sentence—"Live like an artist."

I pondered and journaled what I believe that means. I believe that living like an artist means to create (to bring into form) that which is on your heart for the pure joy and curiosity of its potential beauty and benefit. I realized that there were moments throughout my life when I lived that way, especially when I was younger—drawing, building, and doing gymnastics. Pablo Picasso wrote, "Every child is an artist. The problem is how to remain an artist once we grow up."

I realized that God was telling me to "live" differently, not just "do" differently. For the most part, even though I was engaged in doing what I loved, my motivation had become contaminated by concerns about interest and income, acceptance and appreciation. Living the "way of an artist" would mean I would create and offer simply because God compels me to. "Art is not a thing," Elbert Hubbard wrote. "It is a way." I understand more deeply now what the apostle Paul meant when he said, "To this end I labor, struggling with all his energy, which so powerfully works in me" (Col 1:29).

To live as an artist is to allow whatever it is that "works so powerfully" in you to come out. To refuse to let your glory (your particular splendor, brilliance, abundance) be defined, valued, or constrained by others. To live as an artist means to develop your art through study, training, and experience with whatever time and resources you have, because you love it—not because others are asking for it or you are getting paid for it. Star Richés wrote, "Art is when you hear a knocking from your soul, and you answer."

The term *art* comes from the Greek word *techné*, which actually implies the mastery of any sort of craft. In Latin *art* is *ars,* which means skill or technique with the connotation of beauty. So art is something that you master to the point of beauty—be it photography, questions, music, organization, engaging, speech, colors, encouragement, structure, writing, conciliation, systems, envisioning, or a thousand other things.

We are, after all, God's masterpiece: "For we are God's masterpiece, created in Messiah Jesus to do good works that God prepared long ago to be our way of life" (Eph. 2:10 ISV). We were created to be an artist, to create "good works" as our way of life. This is why the apostle Paul writes, "We ... pray ... that our God might make you worthy of his calling and that through his power he might help you accomplish every good desire and faithful work" (2 Thess. 1:11 ISV).

Live like an artist—offer your glory to the world.

A ROAD LESS TRAVELED ... BUT ONE THAT MUST BE TAKEN

Brilliance, genius, and proficiency in anything take time ... for everyone. If Jesus had to grow "in wisdom and stature [physical maturity], and in favor with God and man" (Luke 2:52), so must we, for "a student is not above his teacher, but everyone who is fully trained will be like his teacher" (Luke 6:40). We must be fully trained to carry out the role we have been given in the Greater Story.

As our intimate ally, God is continually helping us discover more of our glory, developing us into the people who can offer that glory well and bringing us to points of alignment—moments when we must integrate our lives to our desires and to our development.

Scripture offers a beautiful picture of this journey, which the writer refers to as a pilgrimage. "Blessed are those whose strength is in you, who have set their hearts on pilgrimage. As they pass through the Valley of Baca [Weeping], they make it a place of springs; the autumn rains also cover it with pools. They go from strength to strength, till each appears before God in Zion" (Ps. 84:5–7).

We are all on the same journey, the same pilgrimage. We go from strength to increased strength, from glory to increased glory. The path we're on must take us through valleys of weeping as well as places of abundance as we display the glory of God.

That's why we're here. You see—*It's Your Call!*

Notes

Preface

1. Oswald Chambers, *The Philosophy of Sin and Other Studies in the Problems of Man's Moral Life* (Crewe, UK: Oswald Chambers Publications, 1937).

Chapter 1

1. C. S. Lewis, *The Silver Chair* (New York: HarperCollins, 1994), 164.
2. Ibid., 171.
3. J. D. Douglas, *Who's Who in Christian History* (Carol Stream, IL: Tyndale House, 1992), 79.
4. "Going to a Higher Authority," *USA Today,* May 28, 1999.
5. C. S. Lewis, *The Complete C. S. Lewis Signature Classics* (New York: HarperCollins, 2002), 30.
6. Barna Research, "Most People Seek Control, Adventure and Peace in Their Lives," August 1, 2000.
7. Ibid.
8. Russell Baker, quoted in Bob Buford, *Game Plan* (Grand Rapids, MI: Zondervan, 1997), 88.
9. Richard Leider, "Are You Deciding on Purpose," interview by Alan M. Webber, *Fast Company,* January 31, 1998.
10. Oswald Chambers, "November 14," *My Utmost for His Highest:*

Selections for the Year (Grand Rapids, MI: Discovery House, 1993).

11. Theodore Roosevelt, "Citizenship in a Republic," speech at the Sorbonne, Paris, April 23, 1910.

CHAPTER 2

1. Chambers, "August 5," *My Utmost for His Highest: Selections for the Year.*

2. Ibid.

3. C. S. Lewis, *A Grief Observed* (New York: HarperCollins, 2001), 75.

4. Jonathan Swift, "Thoughts on Various Subjects," www.readbookonline.net/readOnLine/3366 (accessed May 27, 2010).

5. Albert Einstein, quoted in Larry Chang, compiler, *Wisdom for the Soul* (Washington, DC: Gnosophia, 2006), 583.

6. Chambers, "June 9," *My Utmost for His Highest: Selections for the Year.*

7. C. S. Lewis, *God in the Dock* (Grand Rapids, MI: Eerdmans, 1994), 65–66.

8. Frederick Buechner, *Now and Then* (New York: HarperCollins, 1991), 87.

CHAPTER 3

1. David Whyte, *The Heart Aroused* (New York: Doubleday, 2002), 19.

2. George MacDonald, *Unspoken Sermons* (Charleston, SC: BiblioBazaar, 2006), 64.

3. Os Guinness, *The Call* (Nashville: Thomas Nelson, 2003), 45.

4. C. S. Lewis, *Letters of C. S. Lewis* (Orlando, FL: Harcourt, 1966), 467.

5. Dallas Willard, *In Search of Guidance* (New York: HarperCollins, 1993), 9

CHAPTER 4

1. C. S. Lewis, *Miracles* (New York: HarperCollins, 2001), 198.

2. Saint Francis of Assisi, "To the Rulers of the People," *The Writings of Saint Francis of Assisi* (1906).

CHAPTER 5

1. John F. Walvoord and Roy B. Zuck, eds., "Daniel 6:10–11," *The Bible Knowledge Commentary (Old Testament)* (Wheaton, IL: Victor Books, 1985).

2. Richard Foster, *The Challenge of the Disciplined Life* (New York: HarperCollins, 1985), 176, 13.

3. Dr. J. Robert Clinton, *Focused Lives* (Altadena, CA: Barnabas Publishers, 1995), 332–89.

4. C. S. Lewis, *An Experiment in Criticism* (Cambridge, UK: Cambridge University Press, 1961), 12.

CHAPTER 6

1. Bill Bright, *The Four Spiritual Laws* (Orlando, FL: Campus Crusade/New Life Publications, 1965).

2. John Boorman and Walter Donohue, eds., *Projections* (London: Faber & Faber, 1992).

3. Chambers, "March 22," *My Utmost for His Highest: Selections for the Year*.

4. Author unknown.

5. C. S. Lewis, *The Lion, the Witch, and the Wardrobe* (New York: HarperCollins, 2000), 142.

6. Ibid., 163.

7. Verse list adapted from Neil T. Anderson, *Victory Over the Darkness* (Ventura, CA: Regal, 2000), 38–39.

CHAPTER 7

1. Aleksandr Solzhenitsyn, *The Oak and the Calf* (London: The Harvill Press, 1997), 109.

2. Oswald Chambers, *The Moral Foundations of Life* (Hants, UK: Marshall, Morgan & Scott, 1966), 9.

3. Adapted from Mike Bickle, various sermons. Used with permission.

CHAPTER 8

1. Robert Louis Stevenson, *An Inland Voyage* (New York: Charles Scribner's Sons, 1895), 22.

2. C. S. Lewis, *Surprised by Joy* (Orlando, FL: Harcourt, 1955), 171.

3. Used with permission.

4. C. S. Lewis, *The Four Loves* (Orlando, FL: Harcourt, 1960), 92.

5. Thomas à Kempis, *The Imitation of Christ* (New York: Cosimo, 2007), 32–33.

CHAPTER 9

1. Erwin McManus, *The Barbarian Way* (Nashville: Thomas Nelson, 2005), 17.

2. "Special Operations," Federation of American Scientists, *The Military Lexicon,* www.fas.org/news/reference/lexicon/mildef.htm (accessed July 2010).

3. Phillips Brooks, *The Purpose and Use of Comfort, and Other Sermons* (New York: E. P. Dutton, 1910), 340.

4. Paul Boller, Jr., *Presidential Anecdotes* (New York: Oxford University Press, 1996), 210–11.

5. Kempis, *The Imitation of Christ,* 53.

6. Lewis, *The Complete C.S. Lewis Signature Classics,* 118.

7. Chambers, "June 25," *My Utmost for His Highest: Selections for the Year.*

8. Chambers, "August 5," *My Utmost for His Highest: Selections for the Year.*

9. C. S. Lewis, *Reflections on the Psalms* (Orlando, FL: Harcourt, 1964), 97.

CHAPTER 10

1. Dan Sullivan, *Focus Your Unique Abilities: The Strategic Coach* (Toronto, Ontario: Strategic Coach, Inc., 1995), 19.

2. James Strong, *The New Strong's Exhaustive Concordance of the Bible* (Nashville: Thomas Nelson, 1996), s.v. "Perseverance."

3. Chambers, "March 22," *My Utmost for His Highest: Selections for the Year.*

Scripture References

All Scripture quotations, unless otherwise noted, are taken from the *Holy Bible, New International Version*®. *NIV*®. Copyright © 1973, 1978, 1984 by International Bible Society. Used by permission of Zondervan. All rights reserved.

Scripture quotations marked AB are taken from *The Amplified Bible*. Copyright © 1954, 1958, 1962, 1964, 1965, 1987 by The Lockman Foundation. Used by permission.

Scripture quotations marked ESV are taken from *The Holy Bible, English Standard Version*. Copyright © 2000; 2001 by Crossway Bibles, a division of Good News Publishers. Used by permission. All rights reserved.

Scripture quotations marked GW are taken from *GOD'S WORD*®. Copyright 1995 God's Word to the Nations. Used by permission of Baker Publishing Group. All rights reserved.

Scripture quotations marked ISV are taken from the *Holy Bible: International Standard Version*®. Copyright © 1996-2008 by The ISV Foundation. All rights reserved internationally. Used by permission.

Scripture quotations marked MSG are taken from *THE MESSAGE*. Copyright © by Eugene H. Peterson 1993, 1994, 1995, 1996, 2000, 2001, 2002. Used by permission of NavPress Publishing Group.

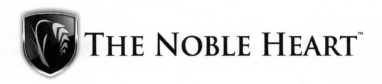

THE NOBLE HEART™

GARY STARTED THE NOBLE HEART WITH THE
PURPOSE OF HELPING MEN AND WOMEN
RECOVER THEIR HEART, WALK WITH GOD,
INTERPRET THEIR LIFE, OFFER THEIR GLORY, AND
PERSEVERE WITH JOY IN ORDER TO LIVE THE
TRANSCENDENT LIFE THEY HAVE BEEN GIVEN.

YOU CAN FIND HIS RETREAT SCHEDULE, SPEAKER
REQUEST FORM, SAMPLE VIDEO CLIPS, E-LETTERS,
PODCASTS, CONTACT INFORMATION, AND
RESOURCES AT WWW.THENOBLEHEART.COM.